ESL Reading Activities

for

Kids and Adults

ESL Reading Activities

for

Kids and Adults

50 Fun Activities for Teaching Reading
Skills to English Language Learners

By Paul Young

ESL Reading Activities for Kids and Adults: 50 Fun Activities for Teaching Reading Skills to English Language Learners / Paul Young

ESL Expat
eslexpat.com

Contents

Introduction

Welcome to *ESL Reading Activities for Kids and Adults*!

Reading skills are the cornerstone of language acquisition, serving as the gateway to understanding, expression, and communication. When learning English as a second language, prioritizing reading skills is essential for learners of all ages and proficiency levels.

By honing their reading abilities, learners not only expand their vocabulary and comprehension but also develop critical thinking skills and cultural awareness.

This activity book features 50 engaging lessons to improve reading skills and help learners enhance their proficiency in English.

Why Focus on Reading Skills?

Reading skills are fundamental to language acquisition and play a crucial role in the development of English proficiency. Mastering reading enables learners to access a vast array of information, broaden their vocabulary, and enhance their comprehension abilities.

Moreover, strong reading skills empower individuals to navigate academic texts, engage with literature, and communicate effectively in real-life situations.

By prioritizing reading skills, learners can unlock countless opportunities for personal growth, academic success, and professional advancement in today's interconnected world.

What to Expect from This Activity Book

A Variety of Activities

Utilize a diverse range of reading materials, such as short stories, newspapers, magazines, essays, screenplays, reviews, blogs, and other online content. Each activity is crafted to engage learners' interest, stimulate critical thinking, and promote vocabulary acquisition.

Practical Application

Engage in activities that mirror real-world reading scenarios, enabling learners to apply their skills in authentic contexts. From analyzing news articles to reading literary texts, learners will develop the ability to comprehend and interpret written English effectively.

Flexible Lessons

This activity book is designed to be versatile and adaptable to various teaching and learning settings. Educators can seamlessly integrate these activities into their lesson plans, classroom activities, or tutoring sessions to supplement existing ESL curricula or provide additional practice opportunities for learners.

Comprehensive Guidelines

Each activity is accompanied by clear instructions and assessment suggestions, facilitating customization to meet the diverse needs of learners. Whether used in formal classroom settings, small group discussions, or self-study environments, learners can enhance their reading skills effectively.

How to Use This Activity Book

This book is designed to be user-friendly and accessible for teachers and students. To maximize its effectiveness, educators can apply the following strategies:

To start, take time to review the layout and organization of the book, including the table of contents and index, to locate activities that align with your teaching objectives and learners' needs.

Next, adapt the activities to suit the proficiency levels, learning styles, and interests of your learners. Prepare the suggested authentic materials, create worksheets, modify the instructions, and consider extension activities to enrich the learning experience. In the print version of this book, use the space at the end of each activity for making notes.

Finally, foster an engaging learning environment where learners feel motivated to actively participate in the reading process. Encourage discussion, critical thinking, and reflection to deepen understanding and promote meaningful interaction with the texts.

By following these strategies, students can enhance their reading ability and other English language skills while interacting with classmates.

Newspaper Articles

Objective: Enhance reading comprehension skills by analyzing newspaper articles and identifying key information.

Level: Intermediate to Advanced

Duration: 60-90 minutes

Materials Needed

- Copies of a local newspaper or access to an online newspaper
- Worksheet with questions related to newspaper articles

Teaching Outline

Introduction (5 minutes)

Start by introducing the activity and its objective: to enhance reading comprehension skills by analyzing newspaper articles. Explain the importance of understanding current events and being able to extract key information from news articles. Emphasize the real-world relevance of the activity.

Instructions (10 minutes)

Divide the class into small groups. Provide each group with a copy of the newspaper or access to an online newspaper website. Distribute worksheets with questions related to newspaper articles to each group. Instruct the groups to complete a newspaper scavenger hunt to find specific types of articles and answer questions about them. Encourage students to work collaboratively within their groups to search for articles and discuss their findings.

Newspaper Analysis (30-45 minutes)

During this phase, instruct the groups to examine the newspapers and answer the questions on their worksheets. Encourage students to read articles carefully and discuss the information they find with their group members.

Group Discussion (10-15 minutes)

Once each group has completed the scavenger hunt and answered all the questions on the worksheet, reconvene as a class. Allow each group to share their findings and discuss the articles they found. Facilitate a discussion about the different types of articles in the newspaper and the importance of reading and understanding current events.

Wrap-Up (5 minutes)

Summarize the key points discussed during the activity. Encourage students to continue reading newspapers regularly to improve their language skills and stay informed about the world around them.

Assessment

Assessment for this activity can be based on students' participation in group discussions, as well as their completion of the worksheet. Teachers can review the completed worksheets to evaluate students' understanding of the articles and their ability to identify key information.

This activity enhances reading comprehension and critical thinking skills. Analyzing real-world texts such as newspaper articles provides insights into different perspectives and writing styles, essential for academic and professional success.

ESL READING ACTIVITIES FOR KIDS AND ADULTS

Magazines

Objective: Improve reading comprehension and critical thinking skills by analyzing articles, advertisements, and other features in magazines.

Level: Intermediate to Advanced

Duration: 60-90 minutes

Materials Needed

- Selection of magazines covering various topics
- Worksheet with questions related to magazine content

Teaching Outline

Introduction (5 minutes)

Introduce the activity by explaining its objective: to develop reading comprehension and critical thinking skills by analyzing articles, advertisements, and other features in magazines. Emphasize the importance of understanding different types of content and the role magazines play in shaping opinions and trends.

Instructions (10 minutes)

Divide the class into small groups. Provide each group with a selection of magazines covering different topics. Distribute worksheets with questions for analyzing magazine content to each group. Instruct the groups to explore the magazines provided and answer the questions on their worksheets. Encourage students to work collaboratively within their groups to analyze articles, advertisements, and other features in the magazines.

Magazine Analysis (30-45 minutes)

During this phase, instruct the groups to examine the magazines and answer the questions on their worksheets. Encourage students to read articles carefully, study advertisements, and explore other features such as editorials, interviews, and reviews. Prompt discussions within the groups to analyze the content and share insights with each other.

Group Discussion (10-15 minutes)

Once each group has completed the analysis and answered all the questions on the worksheet, reconvene as a class. Allow each group to share their findings and discuss the articles, advertisements, and other features they found in the magazines. Facilitate a discussion about the different types of content, writing styles, and persuasive techniques used in magazines.

Wrap-Up (5 minutes)

Summarize the key points discussed during the activity. Encourage students to reflect on the insights gained from analyzing magazine content and consider how they can apply these skills in their daily lives. Remind students to critically evaluate information they encounter in magazines and other media sources.

Assessment

Assessment for this activity can be based on students' participation in group discussions, as well as their completion of the worksheet. Teachers can review the completed worksheets to evaluate students' understanding of the magazine content and their ability to analyze articles, advertisements, and other features.

This activity enhances reading comprehension and critical thinking skills. Analyzing diverse content found in magazines helps students develop a deeper understanding of various topics and perspectives.

Restaurant Menus

Objective: Develop reading and comprehension skills by exploring menus from different restaurants and discussing food options.

Level: Beginner to Intermediate

Duration: 45-60 minutes

Materials Needed

- Menus from various restaurants (printed or digital)
- Worksheet with questions related to menu items and descriptions

Teaching Outline

Introduction (5 minutes)

Introduce the activity by explaining its objective: to improve reading and comprehension skills by exploring menus from different restaurants. Emphasize the importance of understanding menu items and descriptions when dining out or ordering food.

Instructions (5 minutes)

Distribute menus from various restaurants to each student or group. Provide a worksheet with questions related to menu items, descriptions, and categories. Explain the task: students will explore the menus, answer questions, and discuss their findings.

Menu Exploration (30 minutes)

Allow students time to explore the menus provided. Encourage them to read the menu items and descriptions carefully, paying attention to ingredients, prices, and any special features. Prompt students to answer the questions on their worksheets and discuss their responses with their peers.

Group Discussion (10 minutes)

Reconvene as a class and facilitate a group discussion. Allow students to share their findings and discuss interesting menu items they discovered. Encourage students to ask questions and seek clarification on any menu items they found confusing.

Wrap-Up (5 minutes)

Summarize the key points discussed during the activity. Emphasize the importance of understanding menu items and descriptions when dining out. Encourage students to continue exploring menus from different restaurants to expand their vocabulary and cultural knowledge.

Assessment

Assessment for this activity can be based on students' completion of the worksheet and their participation in group discussions. Teachers can

review the worksheets to evaluate students' understanding of menu items and their ability to comprehend written descriptions.

This activity enhances reading and comprehension skills while also introducing students to different cuisines and cultural foods. Analyzing menus helps students expand their vocabulary related to food and dining, as well as their understanding of descriptive language. This activity also promotes cultural awareness and encourages students to explore new foods and dining experiences.

Movie Reviews

Objective: Develop critical thinking skills and enhance reading comprehension by analyzing movie reviews.

Level: Intermediate to Advanced

Duration: 60-75 minutes

Materials Needed

- Collection of movie reviews from newspapers or online sources
- Worksheet with questions related to review content, language use, and critical analysis

Teaching Outline

Introduction (5 minutes)

Begin by explaining the objective of the activity: to develop critical thinking skills and enhance reading comprehension by analyzing movie reviews. Emphasize the importance of understanding different perspectives and evaluating the quality of reviews.

Instructions (5 minutes)

Distribute movie reviews to each student or group. Provide a worksheet with questions related to review content, language use, and critical analysis. Explain the task: students will analyze the movie reviews, answer questions, and discuss their findings with their peers.

Review Analysis (40-50 minutes)

Allow students time to analyze the movie reviews provided. Encourage them to read the reviews carefully, paying attention to the reviewer's opinion, arguments, and supporting evidence. Prompt students to answer the questions on their worksheets and discuss their responses with their peers. Encourage students to consider factors such as the reviewer's credibility and the relevance of their arguments.

Group Discussion (15-20 minutes)

Reconvene as a class and facilitate a group discussion. Allow students to share their findings and discuss interesting aspects of the movie reviews they analyzed. Encourage students to explore different perspectives and interpretations of the same movie. Discuss the importance of critical thinking in evaluating media reviews and forming opinions.

Wrap-Up (5 minutes)

Summarize the key points discussed during the activity. Emphasize the value of critical thinking skills in analyzing movie reviews and making informed decisions about movies to watch. Encourage students to consider multiple sources of information when evaluating media reviews.

Assessment

Assessment for this activity can be based on students' completion of the worksheet and their participation in group discussions. Teachers can review the worksheets to evaluate students' understanding of review content, language use, and critical analysis.

This activity develops critical thinking skills and enhances reading comprehension by providing real-world examples of media analysis. By analyzing movie reviews, students learn to evaluate arguments, consider different perspectives, and form their own opinions about movies. This activity also promotes media literacy and encourages students to approach media consumption with a critical mindset.

Advertisements

Objective: Develop critical thinking skills by analyzing advertisements and understanding persuasive techniques.

Level: Intermediate to Advanced

Duration: 60-75 minutes

Materials Needed

- Collection of advertisements from magazines or online sources
- Worksheet with questions related to advertisement content and persuasive techniques

Teaching Outline

Introduction (5 minutes)

Begin by explaining the objective of the activity: to develop critical thinking skills by analyzing advertisements. Emphasize the importance of understanding persuasive techniques used in advertisements and their impact on consumers.

Instructions (5 minutes)

Distribute a collection of advertisements to each student or group. Provide a worksheet with questions related to advertisement content, target audience, and persuasive techniques. Explain the task: students will analyze the advertisements, answer questions, and discuss their findings with their peers.

Advertisement Analysis (40 minutes)

Allow students time to analyze the advertisements provided. Encourage them to examine the visual elements, language, and appeals used in the advertisements. Prompt students to answer the questions on their worksheets and discuss their responses with their peers. Encourage students to consider the intended message of each advertisement and its effectiveness in persuading consumers.

Group Discussion (15 minutes)

Reconvene as a class and facilitate a group discussion. Allow students to share their findings and discuss the advertisements they analyzed. Encourage students to explore different perspectives and interpretations of the advertisements. Discuss the ethical considerations of advertising and the influence of advertising on society.

Wrap-Up (5 minutes)

Summarize the key points discussed during the activity. Emphasize the value of critical thinking skills in analyzing advertisements and making informed consumer decisions. Encourage students to be mindful of the persuasive techniques used in advertising and to question the messages conveyed by advertisements.

Assessment

Assessment for this activity can be based on students' completion of the worksheet and their participation in group discussions. Teachers can review the worksheets to evaluate students' understanding of persuasive techniques used in advertisements and their ability to analyze advertisement content.

This activity develops critical thinking skills and media literacy by encouraging students to analyze advertisements critically. By examining advertisements, students gain insight into the strategies used by advertisers to influence consumer behavior. This activity also promotes discussion about the role of advertising in society and encourages students to become more discerning consumers.

Recipes

Objective: Enhance reading comprehension and vocabulary skills by reading and analyzing recipes.

Level: Beginner to Intermediate

Duration: 45-60 minutes

Materials Needed

- Selection of recipe books or printed/digital recipes
- Worksheet with questions related to recipe ingredients, instructions, and cooking techniques

Teaching Outline

Introduction (5 minutes)

Begin by explaining the objective of the activity: to improve reading comprehension and vocabulary skills by reading recipes. Emphasize the importance of understanding recipe ingredients, instructions, and cooking techniques when preparing meals.

Instructions (5 minutes)

Distribute recipe books or printed/digital recipes to each student or group. Provide a worksheet with questions related to recipe content, ingredients, and cooking techniques. Explain the task: students will read the recipes, answer questions, and discuss their findings with their peers.

Recipe Reading (30-40 minutes)

Allow students time to read the recipes provided. Encourage them to pay attention to ingredients, measurements, and cooking instructions. Prompt students to answer the questions on their worksheets and discuss their responses with their peers. Encourage students to share personal experiences or tips related to cooking and food preparation.

Group Discussion (10-15 minutes)

Reconvene as a class and facilitate a group discussion. Allow students to share their findings and discuss interesting recipes they discovered. Encourage students to ask questions and seek clarification on any aspects of the recipes they found confusing. Discuss the cultural significance of different recipes and cooking traditions.

Wrap-Up (5 minutes)

Summarize the key points discussed during the activity. Emphasize the importance of understanding recipes when cooking and the role of cultural influences in food preparation. Encourage students to continue exploring recipes from different cuisines to expand their culinary knowledge.

Assessment

Assessment for this activity can be based on students' completion of the worksheet and their participation in group discussions. Teachers can review the worksheets to evaluate students' understanding of recipe ingredients, instructions, and cooking techniques.

This activity enhances reading comprehension and vocabulary skills while also promoting cultural awareness through food. By analyzing recipes, students develop a deeper understanding of cooking techniques and ingredients, as well as cultural traditions related to food preparation. This activity also encourages students to explore new recipes and experiment with cooking, fostering a lifelong appreciation for diverse cuisines.

Transportation Schedules

Objective: Improve reading comprehension and practical language skills by analyzing public transportation schedules.

Level: Beginner to Intermediate

Duration: 45-60 minutes

Materials Needed

- Copies of transportation schedules (bus, train, subway, etc.)
- Worksheet with questions related to schedule information and route planning

Teaching Outline

Introduction (5 minutes)

Begin by explaining the objective of the activity: to improve reading comprehension and practical language skills by analyzing public transportation schedules. Emphasize the importance of understanding schedule information when using public transportation.

Instructions (5 minutes)

Distribute copies of public transportation schedules to each student or group. Provide a worksheet with questions related to schedule information, route planning, and fare prices. Explain the task: students will analyze the schedules, answer questions, and discuss their findings with their peers.

Schedule Analysis (30-40 minutes)

Allow students time to analyze the transportation schedules provided. Encourage them to identify important information such as departure times, arrival times, and route numbers. Prompt students to answer the questions on their worksheets and discuss their responses with their peers. Encourage students to consider factors such as transfer points and travel times when planning routes.

Group Discussion (10-15 minutes)

Reconvene as a class and facilitate a group discussion. Allow students to share their findings and discuss interesting routes or schedule features they discovered. Encourage students to ask questions and seek clarification on any aspects of the schedules they found confusing. Discuss the importance of punctuality and time management when using public transportation.

Wrap-Up (5 minutes)

Summarize the key points discussed during the activity. Emphasize the practical skills gained from analyzing public transportation schedules, such as route planning and understanding schedule information. Encourage students to continue using public transportation as a way to explore their community and improve their language skills.

Assessment

Assessment for this activity can be based on students' completion of the worksheet and their participation in group discussions. Teachers can review the worksheets to evaluate students' understanding of schedule information and their ability to plan routes using public transportation.

This activity enhances reading comprehension and practical language skills by providing real-world context for language learning. By analyzing transportation schedules, students develop practical skills such as route planning and time management. This activity also promotes independence and confidence in using public transportation, which is essential for navigating the community effectively.

Nutrition Labels

Objective: Enhance reading comprehension and critical thinking skills by analyzing nutrition labels.

Level: Intermediate to Advanced

Duration: 60-75 minutes

Materials Needed

- Selection of food product labels with nutrition information
- Worksheet with questions related to label content, serving sizes, and nutritional values

Teaching Outline

Introduction (5 minutes)

Begin by explaining the objective of the activity: to develop reading comprehension and critical thinking skills by analyzing nutrition labels. Emphasize the importance of understanding nutritional information for making informed food choices and promoting healthy eating habits.

Instructions (5 minutes)

Distribute food product labels to each student or group. Provide a worksheet with questions related to label content, serving sizes, and nutritional values. Explain the task: students will examine the nutrition labels, answer questions, and discuss their findings with their peers.

Label Analysis (40-50 minutes)

Allow students time to review the food product labels provided. Encourage them to analyze the serving sizes, ingredient lists, and nutritional values presented on the labels. Prompt students to answer the questions on their worksheets and discuss their responses with their peers. Encourage students to consider the importance of portion control, nutrient density, and ingredient quality in evaluating food products.

Group Discussion (15-20 minutes)

Reconvene as a class and facilitate a group discussion. Allow students to share their interpretations and discuss the main features, strengths, and weaknesses highlighted in the nutrition labels. Encourage students to explore different strategies for interpreting nutritional information and making healthier food choices. Discuss the role of nutrition labels in promoting dietary awareness and supporting public health initiatives.

Wrap-Up (5 minutes)

Summarize the key points discussed during the activity. Emphasize the value of analyzing nutrition labels for developing reading comprehension and critical thinking skills related to food literacy. Encourage students to continue examining food labels and to apply their knowledge in making balanced and nutritious dietary decisions.

Assessment

Assessment for this activity can be based on students' completion of the worksheet and their participation in group discussions. Teachers can review the worksheets to evaluate students' understanding of label content, serving sizes, and nutritional values in food products.

This activity enhances reading comprehension and critical thinking skills by providing practical examples of nutritional information in food products. By analyzing nutrition labels, students gain insight into portion control, nutrient composition, and dietary guidelines. This activity also promotes an understanding of the importance of informed food choices in supporting overall health and well-being.

Real Estate Listings

Objective: Enhance reading comprehension and vocabulary skills by analyzing real estate listings.

Level: Intermediate to Advanced

Duration: 60-75 minutes

Materials Needed

- Collection of real estate listings (printed or digital)
- Worksheet with questions related to property features, prices, and locations

Teaching Outline

Introduction (5 minutes)

Begin by explaining the objective of the activity: to improve reading comprehension and vocabulary skills by analyzing real estate listings. Emphasize the importance of understanding property features, prices, and locations when searching for real estate.

Instructions (5 minutes)

Distribute real estate listings to each student or group. Provide a worksheet with questions related to property features, prices, and locations. Explain the task: students will analyze the real estate listings, answer questions, and discuss their findings with their peers.

Listing Analysis (40-50 minutes)

Allow students time to analyze the real estate listings provided. Encourage them to examine the property features, prices, and locations carefully. Prompt students to answer the questions on their worksheets and discuss their responses with their peers. Encourage students to consider factors such as property size, amenities, and neighborhood characteristics.

Group Discussion (15-20 minutes)

Reconvene as a class and facilitate a group discussion. Allow students to share their findings and discuss interesting properties or listing features they discovered. Encourage students to ask questions and seek clarification on any aspects of the listings they found confusing. Discuss the importance of location and amenities in real estate decision-making.

Wrap-Up (5 minutes)

Summarize the key points discussed during the activity. Emphasize the practical skills gained from analyzing real estate listings, such as understanding property features and prices. Encourage students to continue exploring real estate listings to gain familiarity with the terminology and characteristics of different properties.

Assessment

Assessment for this activity can be based on students' completion of the worksheet and their participation in group discussions. Teachers can review the worksheets to evaluate students' understanding of property features, prices, and locations.

This activity enhances reading comprehension and vocabulary skills by providing real-world examples of real estate terminology and concepts. By analyzing real estate listings, students develop practical skills such as evaluating property features and understanding market trends. This activity also promotes awareness of housing options and encourages students to consider factors such as location and amenities when making real estate decisions.

Short Stories

Objective: Enhance reading comprehension and critical thinking skills by analyzing short stories.

Level: Intermediate to Advanced

Duration: 60-90 minutes

Materials Needed

- Collection of short stories (printed or digital)
- Worksheet with questions related to plot, characters, themes, and literary devices

Teaching Outline

Introduction (5 minutes)

Begin by explaining the objective of the activity: to improve reading comprehension and critical thinking skills by analyzing short stories. Emphasize the importance of understanding plot, characters, themes, and literary devices when interpreting literature.

Instructions (5 minutes)

Distribute short stories to each student or group. Provide a worksheet with questions related to plot, characters, themes, and literary devices.

Explain the task: students will read the short stories, answer questions, and discuss their interpretations with their peers.

Story Analysis (40-50 minutes)

Allow students time to read the short stories provided. Encourage them to analyze the plot, characters, themes, and literary devices carefully. Prompt students to answer the questions on their worksheets and discuss their interpretations with their peers. Encourage students to consider elements such as symbolism, foreshadowing, and irony in their analysis.

Group Discussion (15-20 minutes)

Reconvene as a class and facilitate a group discussion. Allow students to share their interpretations of the short stories and discuss their insights. Encourage students to explore different perspectives and interpretations, fostering critical thinking and literary analysis skills.

Wrap-Up (5 minutes)

Summarize the key points discussed during the activity. Emphasize the importance of critical reading skills in understanding and interpreting literature. Encourage students to continue exploring short stories and to apply their analytical skills to other literary works.

Assessment

Assessment for this activity can be based on students' completion of the worksheet and their participation in group discussions. Teachers can

review the worksheets to evaluate students' understanding of plot, characters, themes, and literary devices in the short stories.

This activity enhances reading comprehension and critical thinking skills by providing students with opportunities to analyze short stories. By examining elements such as plot, characters, themes, and literary devices, students develop a deeper understanding of literature and improve their ability to interpret complex texts. This activity also encourages collaboration and discussion, fostering a supportive learning environment where students can share their insights and perspectives.

Weather Forecasts

Objective: Enhance reading comprehension and critical thinking skills by analyzing weather forecasts.

Level: Beginner to Intermediate

Duration: 45-60 minutes

Materials Needed

- Collection of weather forecasts from newspapers or apps
- Worksheet with questions related to forecast information, terminology, and predictions

Teaching Outline

Introduction (5 minutes)

Begin by explaining the objective of the activity: to enhance reading comprehension and critical thinking skills by analyzing weather forecasts. Emphasize the importance of understanding weather information for daily planning and safety.

Instructions (5 minutes)

Distribute weather forecasts to each student or group. Provide a worksheet with questions related to forecast information, terminology, and predictions. Explain the task: students will analyze the weather forecasts, answer questions, and discuss their findings with their peers.

Forecast Analysis (30-40 minutes)

Allow students time to analyze the weather forecasts provided. Encourage them to examine the forecast information, including temperature, precipitation, wind speed, and atmospheric conditions. Prompt students to answer the questions on their worksheets and discuss their responses with their peers. Encourage students to consider factors such as seasonal trends and weather patterns.

Group Discussion (10-15 minutes)

Reconvene as a class and facilitate a group discussion. Allow students to share their findings and discuss interesting aspects of the weather forecasts they analyzed. Encourage students to compare forecasts from different sources and discuss the accuracy of predictions. Discuss the importance of weather forecasting for various activities and industries.

Wrap-Up (5 minutes)

Summarize the key points discussed during the activity. Emphasize the practical skills gained from analyzing weather forecasts, such as understanding terminology and making informed decisions based on weather information. Encourage students to continue monitoring weather forecasts to stay informed about current and future conditions.

Assessment

Assessment for this activity can be based on students' completion of the worksheet and their participation in group discussions. Teachers can review the worksheets to evaluate students' understanding of forecast information, terminology, and predictions.

This activity enhances reading comprehension and critical thinking skills by providing real-world examples of weather information. By analyzing weather forecasts, students develop practical skills such as interpreting meteorological data and making weather-related decisions. This activity also promotes awareness of weather patterns and phenomena, contributing to students' overall knowledge and preparedness.

Historical Documents

Objective: Develop historical literacy and critical thinking skills by analyzing excerpts from historical documents.

Level: Intermediate to Advanced

Duration: 60-75 minutes

Materials Needed

- Excerpts from historical documents (Declaration of Independence, Treaty of Versailles, WikiLeaks, etc.)
- Worksheet with questions related to content and significance

Teaching Outline

Introduction (5 minutes)

Begin by explaining the objective of the activity: to develop historical literacy and critical thinking skills by analyzing excerpts from historical documents. Emphasize the importance of understanding historical context and interpreting primary sources.

Instructions (5 minutes)

Distribute excerpts from historical documents to each student or group. Provide a worksheet with questions related to document content, context, and significance. Explain the task: students will analyze the historical documents, answer questions, and discuss their findings with their peers.

Document Analysis (40-50 minutes)

Allow students time to analyze the excerpts from historical documents provided. Encourage them to examine the document content, language use, and historical context. Prompt students to answer the questions on their worksheets and discuss their responses with their peers. Encourage students to consider factors such as the author's perspective, audience, and purpose.

Group Discussion (15-20 minutes)

Reconvene as a class and facilitate a group discussion. Allow students to share their findings and discuss the significance of the historical documents they analyzed. Encourage students to explore different interpretations of the documents and consider their impact on historical events and movements. Discuss the importance of primary sources in historical research and understanding.

Wrap-Up (5 minutes)

Summarize the key points discussed during the activity. Emphasize the value of analyzing historical documents for developing critical thinking skills and understanding historical events. Encourage students to continue exploring primary sources to deepen their understanding of history.

Assessment

Assessment for this activity can be based on students' completion of the worksheet and their participation in group discussions. Teachers can review the worksheets to evaluate students' understanding of document content, context, and significance.

This activity develops historical literacy and critical thinking skills by providing real-world examples of primary sources. By analyzing historical documents, students gain insight into the perspectives and motivations of historical figures and events. This activity also promotes an appreciation for the complexity of history and the importance of critically evaluating historical sources.

Interview Transcripts

Objective: Enhance reading comprehension and critical thinking skills by analyzing transcripts of interviews.

Level: Intermediate to Advanced

Duration: 60-75 minutes

Materials Needed

- Transcripts of interviews from podcasts or documentaries
- Worksheet with questions related to interview content, language use, and themes

Teaching Outline

Introduction (5 minutes)

Begin by explaining the objective of the activity: to enhance reading comprehension and critical thinking skills by analyzing transcripts of interviews. Emphasize the importance of understanding spoken language and interpreting interviews in various contexts.

Instructions (5 minutes)

Distribute transcripts of interviews to each student or group. Provide a worksheet with questions related to interview content, language use, and themes. Explain the task: students will analyze the interview transcripts, answer questions, and discuss their findings with their peers.

Transcript Analysis (40-50 minutes)

Allow students time to analyze the transcripts of interviews provided. Encourage them to examine the interview content, language use, and themes discussed. Prompt students to answer the questions on their worksheets and discuss their responses with their peers. Encourage students to consider factors such as the interviewer's questions, the interviewee's responses, and the overall tone of the interview.

Group Discussion (15-20 minutes)

Reconvene as a class and facilitate a group discussion. Allow students to share their findings and discuss the significance of the interviews they analyzed. Encourage students to explore different interpretations of the interviews and consider the perspectives of both the interviewer and interviewee. Discuss the importance of effective communication in interviews.

Wrap-Up (5 minutes)

Summarize the key points discussed during the activity. Emphasize the value of analyzing interview transcripts for developing reading comprehension and critical thinking skills. Encourage students to continue analyzing spoken language in various contexts.

Assessment

Assessment for this activity can be based on students' completion of the worksheet and their participation in group discussions. Teachers can review the worksheets to evaluate students' understanding of interview content, language use, and themes.

This activity enhances reading comprehension and critical thinking skills by providing real-world examples of spoken language. By analyzing interview transcripts, students develop the ability to interpret spoken language, identify key information, and analyze communication dynamics. This activity also promotes an appreciation for the nuances of communication and the importance of effective reading skills in various contexts.

Job Postings

Objective: Develop reading comprehension and career readiness skills by analyzing job postings.

Level: Intermediate to Advanced

Duration: 60-75 minutes

Materials Needed

- Collection of job postings from websites or job boards
- Worksheet with questions related to job requirements, responsibilities, and qualifications

Teaching Outline

Introduction (5 minutes)

Begin by explaining the objective of the activity: to develop reading comprehension and career readiness skills by analyzing job postings. Emphasize the importance of understanding job requirements, responsibilities, and qualifications when searching for employment.

Instructions (5 minutes)

Distribute job postings to each student or group. Provide a worksheet with questions related to job requirements, responsibilities, and qualifications. Explain the task: students will analyze the job postings, answer questions, and discuss their findings with their peers.

Job Posting Analysis (40-50 minutes)

Allow students time to analyze the job postings provided. Encourage them to examine the job requirements, responsibilities, and qualifications in detail. Prompt students to answer the questions on their worksheets and discuss their responses with their peers. Encourage students to consider factors such as desired skills, education level, and experience.

Group Discussion (15-20 minutes)

Reconvene as a class and facilitate a group discussion. Allow students to share their findings and discuss the similarities and differences between the job postings they analyzed. Encourage students to explore different career paths and consider how their skills and interests align with various job opportunities. Discuss the importance of tailoring job applications to meet specific job requirements.

Wrap-Up (5 minutes)

Summarize the key points discussed during the activity. Emphasize the practical skills gained from analyzing job postings, such as understanding job market trends and identifying potential career paths. Encourage students to continue exploring job postings to gain insight into different industries and career opportunities.

Assessment

Assessment for this activity can be based on students' completion of the worksheet and their participation in group discussions. Teachers can review the worksheets to evaluate students' understanding of job requirements, responsibilities, and qualifications.

This activity develops reading comprehension and career readiness skills by providing real-world examples of job opportunities. By analyzing job postings, students gain insight into job market trends, understand employer expectations, and identify potential career paths. This activity also promotes career exploration and helps students make informed decisions about their future employment.

Emails

Objective: Develop professional communication skills and email etiquette by analyzing email correspondence.

Level: Intermediate to Advanced

Duration: 60-75 minutes

Materials Needed

- Sample email correspondence (formal and informal)
- Worksheet with questions related to content, tone, and format

Teaching Outline

Introduction (5 minutes)

Begin by explaining the objective of the activity: to develop professional communication skills and email etiquette by analyzing email correspondence. Emphasize the importance of clear and effective communication in various contexts, including business and personal interactions.

Instructions (5 minutes)

Distribute sample email correspondence to each student or group. Provide a worksheet with questions related to email content, tone, and format. Explain the task: students will analyze the email correspondence, answer questions, and discuss their findings with their peers.

Email Analysis (40-50 minutes)

Allow students time to analyze the email correspondence provided. Encourage them to examine the email content, including greetings, body text, and sign-offs. Prompt students to answer the questions on their worksheets and discuss their responses with their peers. Encourage students to consider factors such as the intended audience, the purpose of the email, and the tone of the communication.

Group Discussion (15-20 minutes)

Reconvene as a class and facilitate a group discussion. Allow students to share their findings and discuss the effectiveness of the email correspondence they analyzed. Encourage students to explore different communication styles and consider how tone and format impact the message's reception. Discuss strategies for writing clear, concise, and professional emails in various contexts.

Wrap-Up (5 minutes)

Summarize the key points discussed during the activity. Emphasize the value of professional communication skills and email etiquette in building positive relationships and achieving communication goals. Encourage students to apply the lessons learned from the email analysis activity to their own email communication practices.

Assessment

Assessment for this activity can be based on students' completion of the worksheet and their participation in group discussions. Teachers can review the worksheets to evaluate students' understanding of email content, tone, and format.

This activity develops professional communication skills and email etiquette by providing real-world examples of email communication. By analyzing email correspondence, students gain insight into effective communication strategies, including tone, clarity, and professionalism. This activity also promotes self-awareness and reflection in students' own email communication practices, leading to improved communication outcomes.

Medical Reports

Objective: Enhance reading comprehension and critical thinking skills by analyzing medical reports.

Level: Advanced

Duration: 60-75 minutes

Materials Needed

- Selection of medical reports (patient charts and diagnostics)
- Worksheet with questions related to report content, structure, and analysis

Teaching Outline

Introduction (5 minutes)

Begin by explaining the objective of the activity: to develop reading comprehension and critical thinking skills by analyzing medical reports. Emphasize the importance of understanding medical terminology, diagnostic procedures, and treatment protocols.

Instructions (5 minutes)

Distribute medical reports on various topics to each student or group. Provide a worksheet with questions related to report content, structure, and analysis. Explain the task: students will read through the medical reports, answer questions, and discuss their findings with their peers.

Report Analysis (40-50 minutes)

Allow students time to read through the medical reports provided. Encourage them to analyze the language, terminology, and findings presented in the reports. Prompt students to answer the questions on their worksheets and discuss their responses with their peers. Encourage students to consider the accuracy of diagnoses, treatment recommendations, and ethical considerations in medical reporting.

Group Discussion (15-20 minutes)

Reconvene as a class and facilitate a group discussion. Allow students to share their interpretations and discuss the main findings, diagnoses, and treatment options presented in the medical reports. Encourage students to explore different perspectives on the medical conditions and to consider the impact of diagnostic methods and treatment approaches on patient care. Discuss the importance of clear and concise reporting in medical communication for effective collaboration among healthcare professionals.

Wrap-Up (5 minutes)

Summarize the key points discussed during the activity. Emphasize the value of analyzing medical reports for developing reading comprehension and critical thinking skills. Encourage students to continue engaging with medical literature and to critically evaluate the evidence presented in medical reports.

Assessment

Assessment for this activity can be based on students' completion of the worksheet and their participation in group discussions. Teachers can review the worksheets to evaluate students' understanding of report content, structure, and analysis.

This activity enhances reading comprehension and critical thinking skills by providing real-world examples of medical documentation. By analyzing medical reports, students gain insight into medical terminology, diagnostic procedures, and treatment modalities. This activity also promotes an understanding of the importance of accurate and thorough reporting in healthcare communication and patient care.

Travel Blogs

Objective: Enhance reading comprehension and cultural awareness by analyzing travel blogs.

Level: Intermediate to Advanced

Duration: 60-75 minutes

Materials Needed

- Selection of travel blogs covering various destinations
- Worksheet with questions related to blog content, language use, and cultural insights

Teaching Outline

Introduction (5 minutes)

Begin by explaining the objective of the activity: to enhance reading comprehension and cultural awareness by analyzing travel blogs. Emphasize the importance of understanding different perspectives and cultural insights when exploring destinations through written narratives.

Instructions (5 minutes)

Distribute travel blog entries to each student or group. Provide a worksheet with questions related to blog content, language use, and cultural insights. Explain the task: students will analyze the travel blog entries, answer questions, and discuss their findings with their peers.

Blog Analysis (40-50 minutes)

Allow students time to analyze the travel blog entries provided. Encourage them to examine the blog content, including descriptions of destinations, experiences, and cultural observations. Prompt students to answer the questions on their worksheets and discuss their responses with their peers. Encourage students to consider factors such as the author's perspective, writing style, and portrayal of cultural differences.

Group Discussion (15-20 minutes)

Reconvene as a class and facilitate a group discussion. Allow students to share their findings and discuss the cultural insights gained from analyzing the travel blog entries. Encourage students to explore different travel experiences and perspectives, reflecting on the diversity of cultures and traditions around the world. Discuss the importance of cultural sensitivity and respectful portrayal of communities in travel writing.

Wrap-Up (5 minutes)

Summarize the key points discussed during the activity. Emphasize the value of analyzing travel blogs for developing reading comprehension skills and cultural awareness. Encourage students to continue exploring diverse perspectives through travel writing and to approach cultural differences with curiosity and respect.

Assessment

Assessment for this activity can be based on students' completion of the worksheet and their participation in group discussions. Teachers can review the worksheets to evaluate students' understanding of blog content, language use, and cultural insights.

This activity enhances reading comprehension and cultural awareness by providing real-world examples of travel narratives. By analyzing travel blogs, students gain insight into different cultures, traditions, and perspectives around the world. This activity also promotes empathy and understanding of cultural diversity, encouraging students to become more informed and culturally sensitive global citizens.

Biographical Profiles

Objective: Develop reading comprehension and critical thinking skills by analyzing biographical profiles of famous figures.

Level: Intermediate to Advanced

Duration: 60-75 minutes

Materials Needed

- Collection of biographical profiles of famous figures
- Worksheet with questions related to biographical content, themes, and significance

Teaching Outline

Introduction (5 minutes)

Begin by explaining the objective of the activity: to develop reading comprehension and critical thinking skills by analyzing biographical profiles s. Emphasize the importance of understanding the lives, achievements, and significance of historical and contemporary figures.

Instructions (5 minutes)

Distribute biographical profiles to each student or group. Provide a worksheet with questions related to biographical content, themes, and significance. Explain the task: students will analyze the biographical profiles, answer questions, and discuss their findings with their peers.

Profile Analysis (40-50 minutes)

Allow students time to analyze the biographical profiles provided. Encourage them to examine the profile content, including key events, achievements, and influences on society. Prompt students to answer the questions on their worksheets and discuss their responses with their peers. Encourage students to consider factors such as the figure's impact on history, relevance to contemporary issues, and portrayal in the media.

Group Discussion (15-20 minutes)

Reconvene as a class and facilitate a group discussion. Allow students to share their findings and discuss the significance of the biographical profiles they analyzed. Encourage students to explore different interpretations of the figures' lives and contributions, considering historical context and cultural perspectives. Discuss the importance of recognizing diverse voices and experiences in biographical narratives.

Wrap-Up (5 minutes)

Summarize the key points discussed during the activity. Emphasize the value of analyzing biographical profiles for developing reading comprehension skills and critical thinking abilities. Encourage students to continue exploring the lives and achievements of famous figures to gain insight into history and human experiences.

Assessment

Assessment for this activity can be based on students' completion of the worksheet and their participation in group discussions. Teachers can review the worksheets to evaluate students' understanding of biographical content, themes, and significance.

This activity enhances reading comprehension and critical thinking skills by providing real-world examples of biographical narratives. By analyzing biographical profiles, students gain insight into the lives, achievements, and significance of historical and contemporary figures. This activity also promotes empathy and understanding of diverse perspectives, encouraging students to appreciate the complexities of human experiences.

Music Lyrics

Objective: Enhance language comprehension and cultural awareness by analyzing music lyrics.

Level: Beginner to Intermediate

Duration: 60-75 minutes

Materials Needed

- Selection of song lyrics covering various genres and themes
- Worksheet with questions related to lyrical content, themes, and cultural references

Teaching Outline

Introduction (5 minutes)

Begin by explaining the objective of the activity: to enhance language comprehension and cultural awareness by analyzing music lyrics. Emphasize the importance of understanding the messages, themes, and cultural references embedded in song lyrics.

Instructions (5 minutes)

Distribute song lyrics to each student or group. Provide a worksheet with questions related to lyrical content, themes, and cultural references.

Explain the task: students will analyze the song lyrics, answer questions, and discuss their findings with their peers.

Lyrics Analysis (40-50 minutes)

Allow students time to analyze the song lyrics provided. Encourage them to examine the lyrical content, including themes, metaphors, and storytelling elements. Prompt students to answer the questions on their worksheets and discuss their responses with their peers. Encourage students to consider factors such as the songwriter's intentions, the song's cultural context, and the emotional impact of the lyrics.

Group Discussion (15-20 minutes)

Reconvene as a class and facilitate a group discussion. Allow students to share their findings and discuss the themes and cultural references present in the song lyrics they analyzed. Encourage students to explore different interpretations of the lyrics and consider how they relate to personal experiences and broader societal issues. Discuss the power of music as a form of expression and communication across cultures.

Wrap-Up (5 minutes)

Summarize the key points discussed during the activity. Emphasize the value of analyzing music lyrics for enhancing language comprehension and cultural awareness. Encourage students to continue exploring diverse musical genres and lyrics to gain insight into different cultures, perspectives, and human experiences.

Assessment

Assessment for this activity can be based on students' completion of the worksheet and their participation in group discussions. Teachers can review the worksheets to evaluate students' understanding of lyrical content, themes, and cultural references.

This activity enhances language comprehension and cultural awareness by providing real-world examples of lyrical narratives. By analyzing music lyrics, students gain insight into the themes, emotions, and cultural influences embedded in songs. This activity also promotes empathy and understanding of diverse perspectives, encouraging students to appreciate the power of music as a universal language of expression.

TED Talk Transcripts

Objective: Develop reading comprehension and critical thinking skills by analyzing TED Talk transcripts.

Level: Intermediate to Advanced

Duration: 60-75 minutes

Materials Needed

- Transcripts of TED Talk presentations covering various topics
- Worksheet with questions related to content, main ideas, and speaker's arguments

Teaching Outline

Introduction (5 minutes)

Begin by explaining the objective of the activity: to develop reading comprehension and critical thinking skills by analyzing TED Talk transcripts. Emphasize the importance of actively engaging with spoken discourse and extracting key information from presentations.

Instructions (5 minutes)

Distribute TED Talk transcripts to each student or group. Provide a worksheet with questions related to content, main ideas, and the speaker's arguments. Explain the task: students will analyze the TED Talk transcripts, answer questions, and discuss their findings with their peers.

Transcript Analysis (40-50 minutes)

Allow students time to analyze the TED Talk transcripts provided. Encourage them to read through the transcripts carefully, identifying main ideas, supporting details, and the speaker's arguments. Prompt students to answer the questions on their worksheets and discuss their responses with their peers. Encourage students to consider the effectiveness of the speaker's delivery and the impact of their message.

Group Discussion (15-20 minutes)

Reconvene as a class and facilitate a group discussion. Allow students to share their findings and discuss the main ideas and arguments presented in the TED Talk transcripts. Encourage students to explore different perspectives and interpretations of the presentations, considering the relevance of the topics to their own lives and communities. Discuss the significance of TED Talks as a platform for sharing ideas and fostering dialogue on global issues.

Wrap-Up (5 minutes)

Summarize the key points discussed during the activity. Emphasize the value of analyzing TED Talk transcripts for developing reading comprehension and critical thinking skills. Encourage students to continue exploring TED Talks and other spoken discourse to broaden their knowledge and perspectives.

Assessment

Assessment for this activity can be based on students' completion of the worksheet and their participation in group discussions. Teachers can review the worksheets to evaluate students' understanding of the TED Talk content, main ideas, and the speaker's arguments.

This activity enhances reading comprehension and critical thinking skills by providing real-world examples of spoken discourse. By analyzing TED Talk transcripts, students gain insight into contemporary issues, innovative ideas, and diverse perspectives. This activity also promotes active engagement with global issues and encourages students to become informed and critical thinkers in today's interconnected world.

Movie Screenplays

Objective: Develop reading comprehension and storytelling analysis skills by analyzing movie screenplays.

Level: Intermediate to Advanced

Duration: 60-75 minutes

Materials Needed

- Selection of movie screenplays
- Worksheet with questions related to screenplay content, structure, and analysis

Teaching Outline

Introduction (5 minutes)

Begin by explaining the objective of the activity: to develop reading comprehension and storytelling analysis skills by analyzing movie screenplays. Emphasize the importance of understanding the structure, dialogue, and stage directions in screenplays.

Instructions (5 minutes)

Distribute movie screenplays to each student or group. Provide a worksheet with questions related to screenplay content, structure, and analysis. Explain the task: students will analyze the screenplays, answer questions, and discuss their findings with their peers.

Screenplay Analysis (40-50 minutes)

Allow students time to analyze the movie screenplays provided. Encourage them to read through the screenplays carefully, paying attention to the dialogue, scene descriptions, and character interactions. Prompt students to answer the questions on their worksheets and discuss their responses with their peers. Encourage students to consider how the screenplay format influences the storytelling and visualization of the movie.

Group Discussion (15-20 minutes)

Reconvene as a class and facilitate a group discussion. Allow students to share their interpretations and discuss the main themes, characters, and plot points presented in the screenplays. Encourage students to explore different interpretations of the screenplays and to consider the impact of effective dialogue and scene descriptions on the viewer's experience. Discuss the role of screenplays in the filmmaking process and their importance in translating written stories into visual narratives.

Wrap-Up (5 minutes)

Summarize the key points discussed during the activity. Emphasize the value of analyzing movie screenplays for developing reading comprehension and storytelling analysis skills. Encourage students to continue exploring different genres of screenplays and to appreciate the artistry and craftsmanship involved in their creation.

Assessment

Assessment for this activity can be based on students' completion of the worksheet and their participation in group discussions. Teachers can review the worksheets to evaluate students' understanding of screenplay content, structure, and analysis.

This activity enhances reading comprehension and storytelling analysis skills by providing real-world examples of movie screenplays. By analyzing screenplays, students gain insight into the structure, dialogue, and visual storytelling techniques used in filmmaking. This activity also promotes an appreciation for the collaborative nature of filmmaking and the importance of effective storytelling in engaging audiences.

Courtroom Transcripts

Objective: Develop critical thinking and analytical skills by analyzing courtroom transcripts.

Level: Advanced

Duration: 60-75 minutes

Materials Needed

- Selection of courtroom transcripts covering various legal cases
- Worksheet with questions related to legal arguments, evidence, and judicial procedures

Teaching Outline

Introduction (5 minutes)

Begin by explaining the objective of the activity: to develop critical thinking and analytical skills by analyzing courtroom transcripts. Emphasize the importance of understanding legal arguments, evidence, and judicial procedures in the context of a courtroom setting.

Instructions (5 minutes)

Distribute courtroom transcripts to each student or group. Provide a worksheet with questions related to legal arguments, evidence, and judicial procedures. Explain the task: students will analyze the courtroom transcripts, answer questions, and discuss their findings with their peers.

Transcript Analysis (40-50 minutes)

Allow students time to analyze the courtroom transcripts provided. Encourage them to read through the transcripts carefully, identifying key legal arguments, evidence presented, and courtroom procedures followed. Prompt students to answer the questions on their worksheets and discuss their responses with their peers. Encourage students to consider the roles of the prosecution, defense, and judge in the legal process.

Group Discussion (15-20 minutes)

Reconvene as a class and facilitate a group discussion. Allow students to share their findings and discuss the legal arguments and procedures presented in the courtroom transcripts. Encourage students to explore different interpretations of the evidence and consider the implications of the legal decisions made. Discuss the importance of the legal system in upholding justice and protecting individual rights.

Wrap-Up (5 minutes)

Summarize the key points discussed during the activity. Emphasize the value of analyzing courtroom transcripts for developing critical thinking and analytical skills. Encourage students to continue exploring legal issues and to consider the ethical and societal implications of legal decisions.

Assessment

Assessment for this activity can be based on students' completion of the worksheet and their participation in group discussions. Teachers can review the worksheets to evaluate students' understanding of legal arguments, evidence, and judicial procedures.

This activity enhances critical thinking and analytical skills by providing real-world examples of legal discourse. By analyzing courtroom transcripts, students gain insight into legal arguments, evidence presentation, and the judicial process. This activity also promotes an understanding of the legal system and its role in resolving disputes and upholding justice in society.

Flight Itineraries

Objective: Enhance reading comprehension and travel planning skills by analyzing flight itineraries.

Level: Beginner to Intermediate

Duration: 60-75 minutes

Materials Needed

- Selection of flight itineraries covering various destinations
- Worksheet with questions related to itinerary details, travel logistics, and airline policies

Teaching Outline

Introduction (5 minutes)

Begin by explaining the objective of the activity: to enhance reading comprehension and travel planning skills by analyzing flight itineraries. Emphasize the importance of understanding itinerary details and airline policies for successful travel planning.

Instructions (5 minutes)

Distribute flight itineraries to each student or group. Provide a worksheet with questions related to itinerary details, travel logistics, and airline policies. Explain the task: students will analyze the flight itineraries, answer questions, and discuss their findings with their peers.

Itinerary Analysis (40-50 minutes)

Allow students time to analyze the flight itineraries provided. Encourage them to review the itinerary details, including flight times, layovers, and airline policies. Prompt students to answer the questions on their worksheets and discuss their responses with their peers. Encourage students to consider factors such as flight connections, travel documentation requirements, and baggage allowances.

Group Discussion (15-20 minutes)

Reconvene as a class and facilitate a group discussion. Allow students to share their findings and discuss the travel logistics and airline policies presented in the flight itineraries. Encourage students to explore different strategies for efficient travel planning and to share personal experiences or tips for navigating air travel. Discuss the importance of careful itinerary review and adherence to airline policies for a smooth travel experience.

Wrap-Up (5 minutes)

Summarize the key points discussed during the activity. Emphasize the value of analyzing flight itineraries for enhancing reading comprehension and travel planning skills. Encourage students to continue practicing travel planning and to seek reliable sources of information when booking flights or making travel arrangements.

Assessment

Assessment for this activity can be based on students' completion of the worksheet and their participation in group discussions. Teachers can review the worksheets to evaluate students' understanding of itinerary details, travel logistics, and airline policies.

This activity enhances reading comprehension and travel planning skills by providing real-world examples of flight itineraries. By analyzing flight itineraries, students gain insight into travel logistics, airline policies, and efficient travel planning strategies. This activity also promotes an understanding of the importance of thorough itinerary review and adherence to airline policies for a successful and stress-free travel experience.

Restaurant Reviews

Objective: Develop reading comprehension and critical thinking skills by analyzing restaurant reviews.

Level: Beginner to Intermediate

Duration: 60-75 minutes

Materials Needed

- Selection of restaurant reviews from various sources
- Worksheet with questions related to review content, culinary aspects, and overall impressions

Teaching Outline

Introduction (5 minutes)

Begin by explaining the objective of the activity: to develop reading comprehension and critical thinking skills by analyzing restaurant reviews. Emphasize the importance of understanding reviews, culinary aspects, and overall impressions for making informed dining choices.

Instructions (5 minutes)

Distribute restaurant reviews to each student or group. Provide a worksheet with questions related to review content, culinary aspects, and overall impressions. Explain the task: students will analyze the restaurant reviews, answer questions, and discuss their findings with their peers.

Review Analysis (40-50 minutes)

Allow students time to analyze the restaurant reviews provided. Encourage them to read through the reviews carefully, identifying key details about the restaurant's cuisine, ambiance, service, and overall dining experience. Prompt students to answer the questions on their worksheets and discuss their responses with their peers. Encourage students to consider factors such as the reviewer's perspective, writing style, and credibility.

Group Discussion (15-20 minutes)

Reconvene as a class and facilitate a group discussion. Allow students to share their findings and discuss the culinary aspects and overall impressions presented in the restaurant reviews. Encourage students to explore different interpretations of the reviews and to consider how they might influence dining decisions. Discuss the importance of critically evaluating restaurant reviews and seeking multiple perspectives before making dining choices.

Wrap-Up (5 minutes)

Summarize the key points discussed during the activity. Emphasize the value of analyzing restaurant reviews for developing reading comprehension and critical thinking skills. Encourage students to continue exploring culinary experiences and to consider their own preferences and priorities when selecting restaurants.

Assessment

Assessment for this activity can be based on students' completion of the worksheet and their participation in group discussions. Teachers can review the worksheets to evaluate students' understanding of review content, culinary aspects, and overall impressions.

This activity enhances reading comprehension and critical thinking skills by providing real-world examples of restaurant reviews. By analyzing restaurant reviews, students gain insight into culinary aspects, service quality, and overall dining experiences. This activity also promotes an understanding of the importance of discerning evaluation and thoughtful consideration when making dining choices.

Car Reviews

Objective: Enhance reading comprehension and critical thinking skills by analyzing car reviews.

Level: Intermediate to Advanced

Duration: 60-75 minutes

Materials Needed

- Selection of car reviews from magazines or websites
- Worksheet with questions related to review content, evaluation criteria, and analysis

Teaching Outline

Introduction (5 minutes)

Begin by explaining the objective of the activity: to develop reading comprehension and critical thinking skills by analyzing car reviews. Emphasize the importance of understanding evaluation criteria, performance metrics, and consumer feedback in assessing vehicles.

Instructions (5 minutes)

Distribute car reviews to each student or group. Provide a worksheet with questions related to review content, evaluation criteria, and analysis. Explain the task: students will read through the car reviews, answer questions, and discuss their findings with their peers.

Review Analysis (40-50 minutes)

Allow students time to review the car reviews provided. Encourage them to analyze the evaluation criteria, performance ratings, and consumer feedback presented in the reviews. Prompt students to answer the questions on their worksheets and discuss their responses with their peers. Encourage students to consider the reliability, safety, comfort, and value propositions of the reviewed vehicles.

Group Discussion (15-20 minutes)

Reconvene as a class and facilitate a group discussion. Allow students to share their interpretations and discuss the main features, strengths, and weaknesses highlighted in the car reviews. Encourage students to explore different perspectives on vehicle performance, design, and market positioning. Discuss the role of consumer reviews in shaping purchasing decisions and influencing automotive industry trends.

Wrap-Up (5 minutes)

Summarize the key points discussed during the activity. Emphasize the value of analyzing car reviews for developing reading comprehension and critical thinking skills. Encourage students to continue exploring automotive literature and to apply critical analysis techniques in evaluating vehicle options and making informed purchasing decisions.

Assessment

Assessment for this activity can be based on students' completion of the worksheet and their participation in group discussions. Teachers can review the worksheets to evaluate students' understanding of review content, evaluation criteria, and analysis of vehicle features and performance.

This activity enhances reading comprehension and critical thinking skills by providing real-world examples of product evaluations in the automotive industry. By analyzing car reviews, students gain insight into consumer preferences, market trends, and product differentiation strategies. This activity also promotes an understanding of the role of consumer feedback and expert opinions in influencing purchasing behavior and brand reputation.

Business Reports

Objective: Develop reading comprehension and critical thinking skills by analyzing business reports.

Level: Advanced

Duration: 60-75 minutes

Materials Needed

- Selection of business reports covering various industries
- Worksheet with questions related to report content, financial terminology, and analysis

Teaching Outline

Introduction (5 minutes)

Begin by explaining the objective of the activity: to develop reading comprehension and critical thinking skills by analyzing business reports. Emphasize the importance of understanding financial terminology and analyzing the content of reports.

Instructions (5 minutes)

Distribute business reports to each student or group. Provide a worksheet with questions related to report content, financial terminology, and analysis. Explain the task: students will analyze the business reports, answer questions, and discuss their findings with their peers.

Report Analysis (40-50 minutes)

Allow students time to analyze the business reports provided. Encourage them to read through the reports carefully, identifying key details about financial data, industry trends, and analysis. Prompt students to answer the questions on their worksheets and discuss their responses with their peers. Encourage students to consider factors such as the report's purpose, data sources, and implications for business decision-making.

Group Discussion (15-20 minutes)

Reconvene as a class and facilitate a group discussion. Allow students to share their findings and discuss the financial data and analysis presented in the business reports. Encourage students to explore different interpretations of the reports and to consider the impact of industry trends on businesses and markets. Discuss the role of business reports in informing stakeholders and guiding strategic decisions.

Wrap-Up (5 minutes)

Summarize the key points discussed during the activity. Emphasize the value of analyzing business reports for developing reading comprehension and critical thinking skills. Encourage students to continue following industry trends and to consider the broader implications of business decisions on stakeholders and the economy.

Assessment

Assessment for this activity can be based on students' completion of the worksheet and their participation in group discussions. Teachers can review the worksheets to evaluate students' understanding of report content, financial terminology, and analysis.

This activity enhances reading comprehension and critical thinking skills by providing real-world examples of business reports. By analyzing business reports, students gain insight into financial data, industry trends, and strategic analysis. This activity also promotes an understanding of the role of business reporting in informing decision-making and guiding organizational strategy.

Scientific Articles

Objective: Enhance reading comprehension and critical thinking skills by analyzing scientific articles.

Level: Advanced

Duration: 60-75 minutes

Materials Needed

- Selection of scientific articles covering various research topics
- Worksheet with questions related to article content, scientific terminology, and analysis

Teaching Outline

Introduction (5 minutes)

Begin by explaining the objective of the activity: to enhance reading comprehension and critical thinking skills by analyzing scientific articles. Emphasize the importance of understanding scientific terminology and analyzing the content of articles.

Instructions (5 minutes)

Distribute scientific articles to each student or group. Provide a worksheet with questions related to article content, scientific terminology, and analysis. Explain the task: students will analyze the scientific articles, answer questions, and discuss their findings with their peers.

Article Analysis (40-50 minutes)

Allow students time to analyze the scientific articles provided. Encourage them to read through the articles carefully, identifying key details about research methods, findings, and analysis. Prompt students to answer the questions on their worksheets and discuss their responses with their peers. Encourage students to consider factors such as the research question, methodology, results, and implications of the research.

Group Discussion (15-20 minutes)

Reconvene as a class and facilitate a group discussion. Allow students to share their findings and discuss the research methods and findings presented in the scientific articles. Encourage students to explore different interpretations of the articles and to consider the broader implications of the research on the field. Discuss the importance of critically evaluating scientific research and considering multiple perspectives.

Wrap-Up (5 minutes)

Summarize the key points discussed during the activity. Emphasize the value of analyzing scientific articles for developing reading comprehension and critical thinking skills. Encourage students to continue exploring scientific literature and to consider the impact of research on society and the scientific community.

Assessment

Assessment for this activity can be based on students' completion of the worksheet and their participation in group discussions. Teachers can review the worksheets to evaluate students' understanding of article content, scientific terminology, and analysis.

This activity enhances reading comprehension and critical thinking skills by providing real-world examples of scientific articles. By analyzing scientific articles, students gain insight into research methods, findings, and analysis in various fields of study. This activity also promotes an understanding of the importance of scientific literacy and critical evaluation of research.

Legal Documents

Objective: Develop reading comprehension and critical thinking skills by analyzing legal documents.

Level: Advanced

Duration: 60-75 minutes

Materials Needed

- Selection of legal documents (contracts and court rulings)
- Worksheet with questions related to document content, legal terminology, and analysis

Teaching Outline

Introduction (5 minutes)

Begin by explaining the objective of the activity: to develop reading comprehension and critical thinking skills by analyzing legal documents. Emphasize the importance of understanding legal terminology and analyzing the content of documents.

Instructions (5 minutes)

Distribute legal documents to each student or group. Provide a worksheet with questions related to document content, legal terminology, and analysis. Explain the task: students will analyze the legal documents, answer questions, and discuss their findings with their peers.

Document Analysis (40-50 minutes)

Allow students time to analyze the legal documents provided. Encourage them to read through the documents carefully, identifying key details about legal clauses, provisions, and implications. Prompt students to answer the questions on their worksheets and discuss their responses with their peers. Encourage students to consider factors such as the purpose of the document, legal rights and responsibilities, and potential implications for stakeholders.

Group Discussion (15-20 minutes)

Reconvene as a class and facilitate a group discussion. Allow students to share their findings and discuss the legal clauses and provisions presented in the documents. Encourage students to explore different interpretations of the documents and to consider the broader legal context. Discuss the importance of understanding legal documents and the role of legal literacy in everyday life.

Wrap-Up (5 minutes)

Summarize the key points discussed during the activity. Emphasize the value of analyzing legal documents for developing reading comprehension and critical thinking skills. Encourage students to continue exploring legal issues and to consider the implications of legal documents on individuals and society.

Assessment

Assessment for this activity can be based on students' completion of the worksheet and their participation in group discussions. Teachers can review the worksheets to evaluate students' understanding of document content, legal terminology, and analysis.

This activity enhances reading comprehension and critical thinking skills by providing real-world examples of legal documents. By analyzing legal documents, students gain insight into legal rights, responsibilities, and implications in various contexts. This activity also promotes an understanding of the importance of legal literacy and critical analysis in navigating legal issues.

Technology Reviews

Objective: Enhance reading comprehension and critical thinking skills by analyzing technology reviews.

Level: Intermediate to Advanced

Duration: 60-75 minutes

Materials Needed

- Selection of technology product reviews
- Worksheet with questions related to review content, technical terminology, and analysis

Teaching Outline

Introduction (5 minutes)

Begin by explaining the objective of the activity: to enhance reading comprehension and critical thinking skills by analyzing technology reviews. Emphasize the importance of understanding technical terminology and analyzing the content of reviews.

Instructions (5 minutes)

Distribute technology product reviews to each student or group. Provide a worksheet with questions related to review content, technical terminology, and analysis. Explain the task: students will analyze the technology reviews, answer questions, and discuss their findings with their peers.

Review Analysis (40-50 minutes)

Allow students time to analyze the technology reviews provided. Encourage them to read through the reviews carefully, identifying key details about product features, performance, and analysis. Prompt students to answer the questions on their worksheets and discuss their responses with their peers. Encourage students to consider factors such as the reviewer's perspective, technical specifications, and real-world usability of the products.

Group Discussion (15-20 minutes)

Reconvene as a class and facilitate a group discussion. Allow students to share their findings and discuss the product features and performance presented in the reviews. Encourage students to explore different interpretations of the reviews and to consider the implications for consumers. Discuss the role of technology reviews in informing purchasing decisions and shaping consumer perceptions.

Wrap-Up (5 minutes)

Summarize the key points discussed during the activity. Emphasize the value of analyzing technology reviews for developing reading comprehension and critical thinking skills. Encourage students to continue exploring technology trends and to consider the broader impact of technology on society and everyday life.

Assessment

Assessment for this activity can be based on students' completion of the worksheet and their participation in group discussions. Teachers can review the worksheets to evaluate students' understanding of review content, technical terminology, and analysis.

This activity enhances reading comprehension and critical thinking skills by providing real-world examples of technology reviews. By analyzing technology reviews, students gain insight into product features, performance, and analysis in various technological domains. This activity also promotes an understanding of the role of consumer reviews in informing purchasing decisions and shaping perceptions of technology.

Famous Quotes

Objective: Enhance reading comprehension and critical thinking skills by analyzing famous quotes.

Level: Beginner to Intermediate

Duration: 60-75 minutes

Materials Needed

- Selection of famous quotes from various sources
- Worksheet with questions related to quote content, interpretation, and analysis

Teaching Outline

Introduction (5 minutes)

Begin by explaining the objective of the activity: to enhance reading comprehension and critical thinking skills by analyzing famous quotes. Emphasize the importance of understanding the meaning of quotes.

Instructions (5 minutes)

Distribute famous quotes to each student or group. Provide a worksheet with questions related to quote content, interpretation, and analysis.

Explain the task: students will analyze the quotes, answer questions, and discuss their findings with their peers.

Quote Analysis (40-50 minutes)

Allow students time to analyze the famous quotes provided. Encourage them to read through the quotes carefully, considering the context, speaker, and underlying message. Prompt students to answer the questions on their worksheets and discuss their responses with their peers. Encourage students to explore different interpretations of the quotes and to consider the broader implications of the messages conveyed.

Group Discussion (15-20 minutes)

Reconvene as a class and facilitate a group discussion. Allow students to share their findings and discuss the meaning and significance of the quotes. Encourage students to explore different perspectives and to consider how the quotes relate to their own experiences and beliefs. Discuss the enduring impact of famous quotes on language, culture, and society.

Wrap-Up (5 minutes)

Summarize the key points discussed during the activity. Emphasize the value of analyzing famous quotes for developing reading comprehension and critical thinking skills. Encourage students to continue exploring quotes from various sources and to consider the power of words in shaping perceptions and inspiring action.

Assessment

Assessment for this activity can be based on students' completion of the worksheet and their participation in group discussions. Teachers can review the worksheets to evaluate students' understanding of quote content, interpretation, and analysis.

This activity enhances reading comprehension and critical thinking skills by providing real-world examples of famous quotes. By analyzing quotes, students gain insight into the context, meaning, and significance of influential statements. This activity also promotes an appreciation for the power of language in conveying ideas and inspiring change.

Speech Transcripts

Objective: Develop reading comprehension and critical thinking skills by analyzing speech transcripts.

Level: Intermediate to Advanced

Duration: 60-75 minutes

Materials Needed

- Selection of speech transcripts from various speakers
- Worksheet with questions related to transcript content, rhetorical devices, and analysis

Teaching Outline

Introduction (5 minutes)

Begin by explaining the objective of the activity: to develop reading comprehension and critical thinking skills by analyzing speech transcripts. Emphasize the importance of understanding rhetorical devices and analyzing the content of speeches.

Instructions (5 minutes)

Distribute speech transcripts to each student or group. Provide a worksheet with questions related to transcript content, rhetorical devices, and analysis. Explain the task: students will analyze the speech transcripts, answer questions, and discuss their findings with their peers.

Transcript Analysis (40-50 minutes)

Allow students time to analyze the speech transcripts provided. Encourage them to read through the transcripts carefully, identifying key themes, arguments, and rhetorical strategies. Prompt students to answer the questions on their worksheets and discuss their responses with their peers. Encourage students to consider factors such as the speaker's purpose, audience, and persuasive techniques.

Group Discussion (15-20 minutes)

Reconvene as a class and facilitate a group discussion. Allow students to share their findings and discuss the themes and rhetorical devices used in the speeches. Encourage students to explore different interpretations of the transcripts and to consider the impact of speeches on audiences and society. Discuss the role of public speaking in shaping public opinion and inspiring action.

Wrap-Up (5 minutes)

Summarize the key points discussed during the activity. Emphasize the value of analyzing speech transcripts for developing reading comprehension and critical thinking skills. Encourage students to continue exploring speeches from various speakers and to consider the power of rhetoric in shaping discourse and driving change.

Assessment

Assessment for this activity can be based on students' completion of the worksheet and their participation in group discussions. Teachers can review the worksheets to evaluate students' understanding of transcript content, rhetorical devices, and analysis.

This activity enhances reading comprehension and critical thinking skills by providing real-world examples of speech transcripts. By analyzing transcripts, students gain insight into the rhetorical strategies used by speakers to convey messages and persuade audiences. This activity also promotes an understanding of the role of public speaking in influencing public opinion and driving social change.

Opinion Columns

Objective: Enhance reading comprehension and critical thinking skills by analyzing opinion columns.

Level: Intermediate to Advanced

Duration: 60-75 minutes

Materials Needed

- Selection of opinion columns from newspapers or magazines
- Worksheet with questions related to column content, argumentation, and analysis

Teaching Outline

Introduction (5 minutes)

Begin by explaining the objective of the activity: to enhance reading comprehension and critical thinking skills by analyzing opinion columns. Emphasize the importance of understanding argumentation techniques and analyzing the content of columns.

Instructions (5 minutes)

Distribute opinion columns to each student or group. Provide a worksheet with questions related to column content, argumentation techniques, and analysis. Explain the task: students will analyze the opinion columns, answer questions, and discuss their findings with their peers.

Column Analysis (40-50 minutes)

Allow students time to analyze the opinion columns provided. Encourage them to read through the columns carefully, identifying the main argument, supporting evidence, and rhetorical strategies used by the author. Prompt students to answer the questions on their worksheets and discuss their responses with their peers. Encourage students to consider the validity of the argument presented and to explore different perspectives on the topic.

Group Discussion (15-20 minutes)

Reconvene as a class and facilitate a group discussion. Allow students to share their findings and discuss the main arguments and persuasive techniques used in the opinion columns. Encourage students to explore different interpretations of the columns and to consider the impact of opinion writing on public discourse. Discuss the role of opinion columns in shaping public opinion and encouraging critical thinking.

Wrap-Up (5 minutes)

Summarize the key points discussed during the activity. Emphasize the value of analyzing opinion columns for developing reading comprehension and critical thinking skills. Encourage students to continue exploring diverse viewpoints and to critically evaluate arguments presented in opinion writing.

Assessment

Assessment for this activity can be based on students' completion of the worksheet and their participation in group discussions. Teachers can review the worksheets to evaluate students' understanding of column content, argumentation techniques, and analysis.

This activity enhances reading comprehension and critical thinking skills by providing real-world examples of opinion writing. By analyzing opinion columns, students gain insight into argumentation techniques and persuasive strategies used by writers to convey opinions and influence readers. This activity also promotes an understanding of the importance of critical evaluation and informed discourse in analyzing opinion writing.

Book Reviews

Objective: Enhance reading comprehension and critical thinking skills by analyzing book reviews.

Level: Intermediate to Advanced

Duration: 60-75 minutes

Materials Needed

- Selection of book reviews from magazines or online sources
- Worksheet with questions related to review content, analysis, and evaluation

Teaching Outline

Introduction (5 minutes)

Begin by explaining the objective of the activity: to enhance reading comprehension and critical thinking skills by analyzing book reviews. Emphasize the importance of understanding the reviewer's perspective and analyzing the content of reviews.

Instructions (5 minutes)

Distribute book reviews to each student or group. Provide a worksheet with questions related to review content, analysis, and evaluation.

Explain the task: students will analyze the book reviews, answer questions, and discuss their findings with their peers.

Review Analysis (40-50 minutes)

Allow students time to analyze the book reviews provided. Encourage them to read through the reviews carefully, considering the reviewer's summary, analysis, and evaluation of the book. Prompt students to answer the questions on their worksheets and discuss their responses with their peers. Encourage students to consider factors such as the reviewer's credibility, writing style, and insights into the book's themes and characters.

Group Discussion (15-20 minutes)

Reconvene as a class and facilitate a group discussion. Allow students to share their findings and discuss the main points and insights presented in the book reviews. Encourage students to explore different perspectives on the book and to consider how reviews can influence readers' perceptions and decisions. Discuss the role of book reviews in promoting literary discussion and shaping readers' interests.

Wrap-Up (5 minutes)

Summarize the key points discussed during the activity. Emphasize the value of analyzing book reviews for developing reading comprehension and critical thinking skills. Encourage students to continue exploring diverse perspectives on literature and to critically evaluate reviews as part of their reading experience.

Assessment

Assessment for this activity can be based on students' completion of the worksheet and their participation in group discussions. Teachers can review the worksheets to evaluate students' understanding of review content, analysis, and evaluation.

This activity enhances reading comprehension and critical thinking skills by providing real-world examples of book reviews. By analyzing book reviews, students gain insight into different perspectives on literature and the elements that contribute to a thoughtful review. This activity also promotes an appreciation for literary discussion and encourages students to critically evaluate reviews as part of their reading experience.

Website Newsletters

Objective: Develop reading comprehension and critical thinking skills by analyzing website newsletters.

Level: Intermediate to Advanced

Duration: 60-75 minutes

Materials Needed

- Selection of website newsletters from various sources
- Worksheet with questions related to newsletter content, structure, and analysis

Teaching Outline

Introduction (5 minutes)

Begin by explaining the objective of the activity: to develop reading comprehension and critical thinking skills by analyzing website newsletters. Emphasize the importance of understanding the purpose and structure of newsletters.

Instructions (5 minutes)

Distribute website newsletters to each student or group. Provide a worksheet with questions related to newsletter content, structure, and analysis. Explain the task: students will analyze the newsletters, answer questions, and discuss their findings with their peers.

Newsletter Analysis (40-50 minutes)

Allow students time to analyze the website newsletters provided. Encourage them to read through the newsletters carefully, considering the main topics, writing style, and layout. Prompt students to answer the questions on their worksheets and discuss their responses with their peers. Encourage students to consider factors such as the target audience, purpose of the newsletter, and effectiveness of the content.

Group Discussion (15-20 minutes)

Reconvene as a class and facilitate a group discussion. Allow students to share their findings and discuss the main themes and elements presented in the newsletters. Encourage students to explore different interpretations of the newsletters and to consider how newsletters engage readers and convey information. Discuss the role of website newsletters in communication and audience engagement.

Wrap-Up (5 minutes)

Summarize the key points discussed during the activity. Emphasize the value of analyzing website newsletters for developing reading comprehension and critical thinking skills. Encourage students to continue exploring different types of newsletters and to consider the impact of effective communication in online platforms.

Assessment

Assessment for this activity can be based on students' completion of the worksheet and their participation in group discussions. Teachers can review the worksheets to evaluate students' understanding of newsletter content, structure, and analysis.

This activity enhances reading comprehension and critical thinking skills by providing real-world examples of website newsletters. By analyzing newsletters, students gain insight into effective communication strategies and audience engagement techniques. This activity also promotes an understanding of the role of newsletters in online communication and information dissemination.

Academic Research Papers

Objective: Develop advanced reading comprehension and critical thinking skills by analyzing academic research papers.

Level: Advanced

Duration: 60-75 minutes

Materials Needed

- Selection of academic research papers from reputable journals
- Worksheet with questions related to paper content, methodology, and analysis

Teaching Outline

Introduction (5 minutes)

Begin by·explaining the objective of the activity: to develop advanced reading comprehension and critical thinking skills by analyzing academic research papers. Emphasize the importance of understanding the structure, methodology, and findings of research papers.

Instructions (5 minutes)

Distribute academic research papers to each student or group. Provide a worksheet with questions related to paper content, methodology, and analysis. Explain the task: students will analyze the research papers, answer questions, and discuss their findings with their peers.

Paper Analysis (40-50 minutes)

Allow students time to analyze the academic research papers provided. Encourage them to read through the papers carefully, considering the research question, methodology, findings, and conclusions. Prompt students to answer the questions on their worksheets and discuss their responses with their peers. Encourage students to critically evaluate the validity of the research and the significance of the findings.

Group Discussion (15-20 minutes)

Reconvene as a class and facilitate a group discussion. Allow students to share their findings and discuss the main themes and findings presented in the research papers. Encourage students to explore different interpretations of the research and to consider the implications of the findings in the broader academic field. Discuss the importance of academic research in advancing knowledge and addressing real-world problems.

Wrap-Up (5 minutes)

Summarize the key points discussed during the activity. Emphasize the value of analyzing academic research papers for developing advanced reading comprehension and critical thinking skills. Encourage students to continue engaging with academic literature and to consider the role of research in informing evidence-based decision-making.

Assessment

Assessment for this activity can be based on students' completion of the worksheet and their participation in group discussions. Teachers can review the worksheets to evaluate students' understanding of paper content, methodology, and analysis.

This activity enhances advanced reading comprehension and critical thinking skills by providing real-world examples of academic research papers. By analyzing research papers, students gain insight into research methodology, data analysis, and scholarly communication. This activity also promotes an understanding of the importance of academic research in contributing to knowledge and addressing societal challenges.

Essays

Objective: Enhance reading comprehension and critical thinking skills by analyzing essays.

Level: Intermediate to Advanced

Duration: 60-75 minutes

Materials Needed

- Selection of essays from various sources
- Worksheet with questions related to essay content, structure, and analysis

Teaching Outline

Introduction (5 minutes)

Begin by explaining the objective of the activity: to enhance reading comprehension and critical thinking skills by analyzing essays. Emphasize the importance of understanding the structure, argumentation, and style of essays.

Instructions (5 minutes)

Distribute essays to each student or group. Provide a worksheet with questions related to essay content, structure, and analysis. Explain the task: students will analyze the essays, answer questions, and discuss their findings with their peers.

Essay Analysis (40-50 minutes)

Allow students time to analyze the essays provided. Encourage them to read through the essays carefully, considering the main argument, supporting evidence, and rhetorical strategies used by the author. Prompt students to answer the questions on their worksheets and discuss their responses with their peers. Encourage students to critically evaluate the effectiveness of the argument and the impact of the essay's message.

Group Discussion (15-20 minutes)

Reconvene as a class and facilitate a group discussion. Allow students to share their findings and discuss the main themes and arguments presented in the essays. Encourage students to explore different interpretations of the essays and to consider how essays engage readers and convey ideas. Discuss the role of essays in expressing personal perspectives and sparking intellectual debate.

Wrap-Up (5 minutes)

Summarize the key points discussed during the activity. Emphasize the value of analyzing essays for developing reading comprehension and critical thinking skills. Encourage students to continue exploring different types of essays and to consider the power of effective writing in conveying ideas and influencing readers.

Assessment

Assessment for this activity can be based on students' completion of the worksheet and their participation in group discussions. Teachers can review the worksheets to evaluate students' understanding of essay content, structure, and analysis.

This enhances reading comprehension and critical thinking skills by providing real-world examples of essays. By analyzing essays, students gain insight into argumentation techniques, rhetorical strategies, and the art of persuasion. This activity also promotes an appreciation for the diversity of perspectives and ideas expressed through essays and encourages students to engage critically with written texts.

Resumes

Objective: Develop critical reading skills by analyzing resumes.

Level: Intermediate to Advanced

Duration: 60-75 minutes

Materials Needed

- Selection of resumes from online sources and job websites
- Worksheet with questions related to resume content, structure, and analysis

Teaching Outline

Introduction (5 minutes)

Begin by explaining the objective of the activity: to develop critical reading skills by analyzing resumes. Emphasize the importance of understanding the structure, content, and formatting of resumes.

Instructions (5 minutes)

Distribute resumes to each student or group. Provide a worksheet with questions related to resume content, structure, and analysis. Explain the task: students will analyze the resumes, answer questions, and discuss their findings with their peers.

Resume Analysis (40-50 minutes)

Allow students time to analyze the resumes provided. Encourage them to read through the resumes carefully, considering the candidate's qualifications, skills, and experiences. Prompt students to answer the questions on their worksheets and discuss their responses with their peers. Encourage students to critically evaluate the effectiveness of the resume in presenting the candidate's profile and qualifications.

Group Discussion (15-20 minutes)

Reconvene as a class and facilitate a group discussion. Allow students to share their findings and discuss the main strengths and weaknesses presented in the resumes. Encourage students to explore different perspectives on resume writing and to consider the importance of tailoring resumes to specific job opportunities. Discuss the role of resumes in the job application process and the impact of effective resume writing on career prospects.

Wrap-Up (5 minutes)

Summarize the key points discussed during the activity. Emphasize the value of analyzing resumes for developing critical reading skills and understanding the job application process. Encourage students to continue exploring different resume formats and to consider the importance of presenting themselves effectively in professional contexts.

Assessment

Assessment for this activity can be based on students' completion of the worksheet and their participation in group discussions. Teachers can review the worksheets to evaluate students' understanding of resume content, structure, and analysis.

This enhances critical reading skills by providing real-world examples of resumes. By analyzing resumes, students gain insight into the elements of effective resume writing, including content organization, language use, and formatting. This activity also promotes an understanding of the importance of presenting oneself effectively in professional contexts and prepares students for future career opportunities.

Classic Poems

Objective: Enhance literary analysis skills by analyzing classic poems.

Level: Intermediate to Advanced

Duration: 60-75 minutes

Materials Needed

- Selection of classic poems from renowned poets (Shakespeare, Wordsworth, Dickinson, etc.)
- Worksheet with questions related to poem content, structure, and analysis

Teaching Outline

Introduction (5 minutes)

Begin by explaining the objective of the activity: to enhance literary analysis skills by analyzing classic poems. Emphasize the importance of understanding the themes, imagery, and literary devices used in poetry.

Instructions (5 minutes)

Distribute classic poems to each student or group. Provide a worksheet with questions related to poem content, structure, and analysis. Explain the task: students will analyze the poems, answer questions, and discuss their findings with their peers.

Poem Analysis (40-50 minutes)

Allow students time to analyze the classic poems provided. Encourage them to read through the poems carefully, considering the poet's use of language, imagery, and poetic techniques. Prompt students to answer the questions on their worksheets and discuss their responses with their peers. Encourage students to delve into the deeper meanings and interpretations of the poems.

Group Discussion (15-20 minutes)

Reconvene as a class and facilitate a group discussion. Allow students to share their interpretations and discuss the main themes and literary devices presented in the poems. Encourage students to explore different perspectives on the poems and to consider the impact of poetic language and imagery on the reader. Discuss the enduring relevance of classic poetry and its ability to evoke emotions and provoke thought.

Wrap-Up (5 minutes)

Summarize the key points discussed during the activity. Emphasize the value of analyzing classic poems for developing literary analysis skills and understanding the beauty and complexity of poetry. Encourage students to continue exploring classic poetry and to engage critically with works of literature.

Assessment

Assessment for this activity can be based on students' completion of the worksheet and their participation in group discussions. Teachers can review the worksheets to evaluate students' understanding of poem content, structure, and analysis.

This activity enhances literary analysis skills by providing real-world examples of classic poems. By analyzing poems, students gain insight into the use of language, imagery, and poetic techniques to convey meaning and evoke emotions. This activity also promotes an appreciation for the richness and diversity of poetic expression across different time periods and cultures.

Event Announcements

Objective: Develop reading comprehension and critical thinking skills by analyzing event announcements.

Level: Beginner to Intermediate

Duration: 60-75 minutes

Materials Needed

- Selection of event announcements on websites and social media
- Worksheet with questions related to announcement content, structure, and analysis

Teaching Outline

Introduction (5 minutes)

Begin by explaining the objective of the activity: to develop reading comprehension and critical thinking skills by analyzing event announcements. Emphasize the importance of understanding the purpose, audience, and key information in event announcements.

Instructions (5 minutes)

Distribute event announcements to each student or group. Provide a worksheet with questions related to announcement content, structure, and analysis. Explain the task: students will analyze the announcements, answer questions, and discuss their findings with their peers.

Event Announcement Analysis (40-50 minutes)

Allow students time to analyze the event announcements provided. Encourage them to read through the announcements carefully, considering the event details, target audience, and persuasive techniques used. Prompt students to answer the questions on their worksheets and discuss their responses with their peers. Encourage students to critically evaluate the effectiveness of the announcements in attracting and informing potential attendees.

Group Discussion (15-20 minutes)

Reconvene as a class and facilitate a group discussion. Allow students to share their findings and discuss the main features and strategies presented in the announcements. Encourage students to explore different interpretations of the announcements and to consider the impact of effective event promotion on audience engagement. Discuss the role of event announcements in informing and engaging communities and promoting cultural events.

Wrap-Up (5 minutes)

Summarize the key points discussed during the activity. Emphasize the value of analyzing event announcements for developing reading comprehension and critical thinking skills. Encourage students to continue exploring different types of announcements and to consider the importance of effective communication in event promotion.

Assessment

Assessment for this activity can be based on students' completion of the worksheet and their participation in group discussions. Teachers can review the worksheets to evaluate students' understanding of announcement content, structure, and analysis.

This activity enhances reading comprehension and critical thinking skills by providing real-world examples of event announcements. By analyzing announcements, students gain insight into effective communication strategies and audience engagement techniques. This activity also promotes an understanding of the role of event announcements in promoting cultural events and fostering community participation.

Comic Books

Objective: Enhance reading comprehension and visual literacy skills by analyzing comic books.

Level: Beginner to Intermediate

Duration: 60-75 minutes

Materials Needed

- Selection of comic books or graphic novels
- Worksheet with questions related to comic book content, structure, and analysis

Teaching Outline

Introduction (5 minutes)

Begin by explaining the objective of the activity: to enhance reading comprehension and visual literacy skills by analyzing comic books. Emphasize the unique combination of text and visuals in comic books and the importance of understanding both.

Instructions (5 minutes)

Distribute comic books or graphic novels to each student or group. Provide a worksheet with questions related to comic book content, structure, and analysis. Explain the task: students will analyze the comic books, answer questions, and discuss their findings with their peers.

Comic Book Analysis (40-50 minutes)

Allow students time to analyze the comic books provided. Encourage them to read through the comic books carefully, paying attention to both the text and visuals. Prompt students to answer the questions on their worksheets and discuss their responses with their peers. Encourage students to consider how the combination of text and visuals contributes to the storytelling and meaning of the comic book.

Group Discussion (15-20 minutes)

Reconvene as a class and facilitate a group discussion. Allow students to share their interpretations and discuss the main themes, characters, and visual elements presented in the comic books. Encourage students to explore different interpretations of the comic books and to consider the impact of visual storytelling techniques on reader engagement. Discuss the unique features of comic books as a literary form and their cultural significance.

Wrap-Up (5 minutes)

Summarize the key points discussed during the activity. Emphasize the value of analyzing comic books for developing reading comprehension and visual literacy skills. Encourage students to continue exploring different genres of comic books and graphic novels and to appreciate the creativity and artistry involved in their creation.

Assessment

Assessment for this activity can be based on students' completion of the worksheet and their participation in group discussions. Teachers can review the worksheets to evaluate students' understanding of comic book content, structure, and analysis.

This activity enhances reading comprehension and visual literacy skills by providing real-world examples of comic books. By analyzing comic books, students gain insight into the unique storytelling techniques and artistic elements of the medium. This activity also promotes an appreciation for the creativity and diversity of comic book genres and their ability to engage readers of all ages.

Google Maps

Objective: Enhance reading comprehension and geographical knowledge by analyzing Google Maps.

Level: Beginner to Intermediate

Duration: 45-60 minutes

Materials Needed

- Access to computers or devices with internet connection
- Worksheet with questions related to map features, locations, and directions

Teaching Outline

Introduction (5 minutes)

Begin by explaining the objective of the activity: to improve reading comprehension and geographical knowledge by analyzing Google Maps. Emphasize the importance of map-reading skills in navigating the world and understanding geographic features.

Instructions (5 minutes)

Divide the class into small groups and provide each group with access to computers, tablets, or smartphones with internet connection.

Distribute a worksheet with questions related to map features, locations, and directions. Explain the task: students will explore Google Maps, answer questions, and discuss their findings with their group members.

Map Exploration (30-40 minutes)

Allow students time to explore Google Maps and navigate to different locations. Encourage them to examine map features such as landmarks, roads, and geographical features. Prompt students to answer the questions on their worksheets and discuss their observations with their group members. Encourage students to explore different regions and zoom levels on the map for a comprehensive understanding.

Group Discussion (10-15 minutes)

Reconvene as a class and facilitate a group discussion. Allow each group to share their findings and discuss interesting locations or features they discovered on Google Maps. Encourage students to ask questions and seek clarification on any aspects of the map they found confusing. Discuss the importance of map-reading skills in everyday life and various applications, such as travel and navigation.

Wrap-Up (5 minutes)

Summarize the key points discussed during the activity. Emphasize the practical skills gained from analyzing Google Maps, such as understanding geographical features and navigating unfamiliar locations. Encourage students to continue exploring Google Maps to enhance their geographical knowledge and map-reading skills.

Assessment

Assessment for this activity can be based on students' completion of the worksheet and their participation in group discussions. Teachers can review the worksheets to evaluate students' understanding of map features, locations, and directions on Google Maps.

This activity enhances reading comprehension and geographical knowledge by providing students with opportunities to analyze Google Maps. By exploring map features, locations, and directions, students develop a deeper understanding of geography and improve their map-reading skills. This activity also encourages collaboration and discussion, fostering a supportive learning environment where students can share their observations and insights on geographic features.

Movie Subtitles

Objective: Develop reading comprehension and language proficiency by analyzing movie subtitles.

Level: Beginner to Intermediate

Duration: 60-75 minutes

Materials Needed

- Selection of movie clips with subtitles
- Worksheet with questions related to subtitle content, structure, and analysis

Teaching Outline

Introduction (5 minutes)

Begin by explaining the objective of the activity: to develop reading comprehension and language proficiency by analyzing movie subtitles. Emphasize the importance of understanding the language, context, and cultural references in subtitles.

Instructions (5 minutes)

Distribute movie clips with subtitles to each student or group. Provide a worksheet with questions related to subtitle content, structure, and analysis. Explain the task: students will watch the movie clips, read the subtitles, answer questions, and discuss their findings with their peers.

Subtitle Analysis (40-50 minutes)

Allow students time to watch the movie clips with subtitles provided. Encourage them to read through the subtitles carefully, paying attention to the dialogue, translation, and synchronization with the movie scenes. Prompt students to answer the questions on their worksheets and discuss their responses with their peers. Encourage students to consider the nuances of language, cultural references, and linguistic choices reflected in the subtitles.

Group Discussion (15-20 minutes)

Reconvene as a class and facilitate a group discussion. Allow students to share their interpretations and discuss the main themes, language usage, and translation challenges presented in the subtitles. Encourage students to explore different interpretations of the subtitles and to consider the impact of cultural differences on language translation. Discuss the role of subtitles in language learning and cross-cultural communication.

Wrap-Up (5 minutes)

Summarize the key points discussed during the activity. Emphasize the value of analyzing movie subtitles for developing reading comprehension and language proficiency. Encourage students to continue practicing with subtitles in movies and other media to enhance their language skills and cultural awareness.

Assessment

Assessment for this activity can be based on students' completion of the worksheet and their participation in group discussions. Teachers can review the worksheets to evaluate students' understanding of subtitle content, structure, and analysis.

This activity enhances reading comprehension and language proficiency by providing real-world examples of subtitles. By analyzing subtitles, students gain insight into language usage, translation techniques, and cultural nuances. This activity also promotes an appreciation for the role of subtitles in language learning and cross-cultural communication.

Social Media Comments

Objective: Develop reading comprehension and critical thinking skills by analyzing social media comments.

Level: Beginner to Intermediate

Duration: 60-75 minutes

Materials Needed

- Selection of social media posts with comments
- Worksheet with questions related to comment content, structure, and analysis

Teaching Outline

Introduction (5 minutes)

Begin by explaining the objective of the activity: to develop reading comprehension and critical thinking skills by analyzing social media comments. Emphasize the importance of understanding the language, tone, and context of online comments.

Instructions (5 minutes)

Distribute social media posts with comments to each student or group. Provide a worksheet with questions related to comment content, structure, and analysis. Explain the task: students will read through the social media comments, answer questions, and discuss their findings with their peers.

Comment Analysis (40-50 minutes)

Allow students time to read through the social media posts and comments provided. Encourage them to analyze the language, tone, and arguments presented in the comments. Prompt students to answer the questions on their worksheets and discuss their responses with their peers. Encourage students to consider the different perspectives and viewpoints expressed in the comments.

Group Discussion (15-20 minutes)

Reconvene as a class and facilitate a group discussion. Allow students to share their interpretations and discuss the main themes, arguments, and communication styles presented in the social media comments. Encourage students to explore different interpretations of the comments and to consider the impact of online communication on public discourse and understanding. Discuss the role of social media in facilitating discussion and information sharing.

Wrap-Up (5 minutes)

Summarize the key points discussed during the activity. Emphasize the value of analyzing social media comments for developing reading comprehension and critical thinking skills. Encourage students to continue engaging with online discussions and to critically evaluate the information and perspectives presented.

Assessment

Assessment for this activity can be based on students' completion of the worksheet and their participation in group discussions. Teachers can review the worksheets to evaluate students' understanding of comment content, structure, and analysis.

This activity enhances reading comprehension and critical thinking skills by providing real-world examples of online comments. By analyzing social media comments, students gain insight into different communication styles, argumentation techniques, and online discourse. This activity also promotes an understanding of the role of social media in shaping public opinion and fostering dialogue.

Wikipedia Pages

Objective: Enhance reading comprehension and critical thinking skills by analyzing Wikipedia pages.

Level: Intermediate to Advanced

Duration: 60-75 minutes

Materials Needed

- Selection of Wikipedia pages on various topics
- Worksheet with questions related to page content, structure, and analysis

Teaching Outline

Introduction (5 minutes)

Begin by explaining the objective of the activity: to develop reading comprehension and critical thinking skills by analyzing Wikipedia pages. Emphasize the importance of understanding the language, tone, and structure of Wikipedia articles.

Instructions (5 minutes)

Distribute Wikipedia pages on different topics to each student or group. Provide a worksheet with questions related to page content, structure, and analysis. Explain the task: students will read through the Wikipedia pages, answer questions, and discuss their findings with their peers.

Page Analysis (40-50 minutes)

Allow students time to read through the Wikipedia pages provided. Encourage them to analyze the language, tone, and information presented in the articles. Prompt students to answer the questions on their worksheets and discuss their responses with their peers. Encourage students to consider the reliability of the sources cited, the neutrality of the content, and the overall organization of the pages.

Group Discussion (15-20 minutes)

Reconvene as a class and facilitate a group discussion. Allow students to share their interpretations and discuss the main themes, arguments, and presentation styles presented in the Wikipedia pages. Encourage students to explore different perspectives on the topics and to consider the impact of Wikipedia as a source of information. Discuss the role of Wikipedia in knowledge dissemination and the importance of critical evaluation of online sources.

Wrap-Up (5 minutes)

Summarize the key points discussed during the activity. Emphasize the value of analyzing Wikipedia pages for developing reading comprehension and critical thinking skills. Encourage students to continue engaging with diverse sources of information and to critically evaluate the content they encounter.

Assessment

Assessment for this activity can be based on students' completion of the worksheet and their participation in group discussions. Teachers can review the worksheets to evaluate students' understanding of page content, structure, and analysis.

This activity enhances reading comprehension and critical thinking skills by providing real-world examples of informational articles. By analyzing Wikipedia pages, students gain insight into different writing styles, content organization, and information presentation techniques. This activity also promotes an understanding of the importance of critical evaluation and cross-referencing of online sources.

Sports Statistics

Objective: Enhance reading comprehension and critical thinking skills by analyzing sports statistics.

Level: Beginner to Intermediate

Duration: 60-75 minutes

Materials Needed

- Selection of sports statistics (game summaries or player stats)
- Worksheet with questions related to statistical analysis, trends, and insights

Teaching Outline

Introduction (5 minutes)

Begin by explaining the objective of the activity: to develop reading comprehension and critical thinking skills by analyzing sports statistics. Emphasize the importance of understanding statistical measures, trends, and performance metrics for comprehensive analysis in sports.

Instructions (5 minutes)

Distribute sports statistics tables or reports to each student or group. Provide a worksheet with questions related to statistical analysis, trends, and insights. Explain the task: students will review the sports statistics provided, answer questions, and discuss their findings with their peers.

Statistics Analysis (40-50 minutes)

Allow students time to review the sports statistics provided. Encourage them to analyze the numerical data, trends, and patterns presented in the statistics. Prompt students to answer the questions on their worksheets and discuss their responses with their peers. Encourage students to consider the significance of key performance indicators, player comparisons, and team strategies reflected in the statistics.

Group Discussion (15-20 minutes)

Reconvene as a class and facilitate a group discussion. Allow students to share their interpretations and discuss the main trends, insights, and implications derived from the sports statistics. Encourage students to explore different perspectives on player and team performance and to consider the impact of statistical analysis on coaching decisions and fan engagement. Discuss the importance of data-driven decision-making in sports management and the media.

Wrap-Up (5 minutes)

Summarize the key points discussed during the activity. Emphasize the value of analyzing sports statistics for developing reading comprehension and critical thinking skills. Encourage students to continue exploring sports data and to apply statistical analysis techniques in evaluating athletic performance and strategic outcomes.

Assessment

Assessment for this activity can be based on students' completion of the worksheet and their participation in group discussions. Teachers can review the worksheets to evaluate students' understanding of statistical analysis, trends, and insights derived from sports statistics.

This activity enhances reading comprehension and critical thinking skills by providing real-world examples of statistical analysis in sports. By analyzing sports statistics, students gain insight into data interpretation, trend analysis, and performance evaluation in athletic contexts. This activity also promotes an understanding of the role of statistical literacy in sports journalism, coaching, and sports management decision-making.

Product Manuals

Objective: Enhance reading comprehension and critical thinking skills by analyzing product manuals.

Level: Intermediate to Advanced

Duration: 60-75 minutes

Materials Needed

- Selection of product manuals for different products
- Worksheet with questions related to manual content, structure, and analysis

Teaching Outline

Introduction (5 minutes)

Begin by explaining the objective of the activity: to develop reading comprehension and critical thinking skills by analyzing product manuals. Emphasize the importance of understanding the language, format, and instructions provided in product manuals.

Instructions (5 minutes)

Distribute product manuals for different products to each student or group. Provide a worksheet with questions related to manual content, structure, and analysis. Explain the task: students will read through the product manuals, answer questions, and discuss their findings with their peers.

Manual Analysis (40-50 minutes)

Allow students time to read through the product manuals provided. Encourage them to analyze the language, format, and instructions presented in the manuals. Prompt students to answer the questions on their worksheets and discuss their responses with their peers. Encourage students to consider the clarity of instructions, use of diagrams or illustrations, and organization of information in the manuals.

Group Discussion (15-20 minutes)

Reconvene as a class and facilitate a group discussion. Allow students to share their interpretations and discuss the main features, functions, and usability of the products based on the manuals. Encourage students to explore different interpretations of the instructions and to consider the effectiveness of the manuals in guiding users. Discuss the importance of clear and concise communication in product manuals for consumer satisfaction.

Wrap-Up (5 minutes)

Summarize the key points discussed during the activity. Emphasize the value of analyzing product manuals for developing reading comprehension and critical thinking skills. Encourage students to apply the skills learned to effectively navigate and utilize product manuals in real-life situations.

Assessment

Assessment for this activity can be based on students' completion of the worksheet and their participation in group discussions. Teachers can review the worksheets to evaluate students' understanding of manual content, structure, and analysis.

This activity enhances reading comprehension and critical thinking skills by providing real-world examples of instructional texts. By analyzing product manuals, students gain insight into effective communication strategies, technical writing conventions, and user interface design. This activity also promotes an understanding of the importance of clear and user-friendly documentation in product usage.

Medical Prescriptions

Objective: Enhance reading comprehension and critical thinking skills by analyzing medical prescriptions.

Level: Intermediate to Advanced

Duration: 60-75 minutes

Materials Needed

- Selection of medical prescriptions (real or simulated)
- Worksheet with questions related to prescription content, dosage instructions, and analysis

Teaching Outline

Introduction (5 minutes)

Begin by explaining the objective of the activity: to develop reading comprehension and critical thinking skills by analyzing medical prescriptions. Emphasize the importance of understanding dosage instructions and patient safety considerations in medical prescriptions.

Instructions (5 minutes)

Distribute medical prescriptions to each student or group. Provide a worksheet with questions related to prescription content, dosage instructions, and analysis. Explain the task: students will review the medical prescriptions, answer questions, and discuss their findings with their peers.

Prescription Analysis (40-50 minutes)

Allow students time to review the medical prescriptions provided. Encourage them to analyze the medication names, dosage instructions, frequency of administration, and any special instructions or warnings. Prompt students to answer the questions on their worksheets and discuss their responses with their peers. Encourage students to consider the appropriateness of the prescribed medications for the indicated conditions and potential adverse effects or drug interactions.

Group Discussion (15-20 minutes)

Reconvene as a class and facilitate a group discussion. Allow students to share their interpretations and discuss the main components and considerations in the medical prescriptions. Encourage students to explore different perspectives on medication management and to consider the role of healthcare providers in ensuring patient safety and adherence to treatment regimens. Discuss the importance of clear communication between healthcare professionals and patients in prescription writing and medication management.

Wrap-Up (5 minutes)

Summarize the key points discussed during the activity. Emphasize the value of analyzing medical prescriptions for developing reading comprehension and critical thinking skills. Encourage students to apply the skills learned to interpret and follow medical prescriptions accurately in real-life situations.

Assessment

Assessment for this activity can be based on students' completion of the worksheet and their participation in group discussions. Teachers can review the worksheets to evaluate students' understanding of prescription content, dosage instructions, and analysis.

This activity enhances reading comprehension and critical thinking skills by providing real-world examples of medical prescriptions. By analyzing medical prescriptions, students gain insight into medication management, dosage calculations, and patient safety considerations. This activity also promotes an understanding of the importance of clear and accurate communication in medical practice for effective patient care.

Stock Market Reports

Objective: Enhance reading comprehension and critical thinking skills by analyzing stock market reports.

Level: Advanced

Duration: 60-75 minutes

Materials Needed

- Selection of stock market reports (from newspapers or online)
- Worksheet with questions related to report content, trends, and analysis

Teaching Outline

Introduction (5 minutes)

Begin by explaining the objective of the activity: to develop reading comprehension and critical thinking skills by analyzing stock market reports. Emphasize the importance of understanding financial terminology, market trends, and investment strategies.

Instructions (5 minutes)

Distribute stock market reports to each student or group. Provide a worksheet with questions related to report content, market trends, and analysis. Explain the task: students will read through the stock market reports, answer questions, and discuss their findings with their peers.

Report Analysis (40-50 minutes)

Allow students time to review the stock market reports provided. Encourage them to analyze the market trends, performance indicators, and investment recommendations presented in the reports. Prompt students to answer the questions on their worksheets and discuss their responses with their peers. Encourage students to consider the factors influencing market fluctuations, risk management strategies, and potential investment opportunities.

Group Discussion (15-20 minutes)

Reconvene as a class and facilitate a group discussion. Allow students to share their interpretations and discuss the main trends, predictions, and investment strategies presented in the stock market reports. Encourage students to explore different perspectives on market analysis and to consider the impact of economic indicators and geopolitical events on stock market performance. Discuss the importance of informed decision-making and risk assessment in financial management.

Wrap-Up (5 minutes)

Summarize the key points discussed during the activity. Emphasize the value of analyzing stock market reports for developing reading comprehension and critical thinking skills. Encourage students to continue monitoring market trends and to apply analytical skills in making informed investment decisions.

Assessment

Assessment for this activity can be based on students' completion of the worksheet and their participation in group discussions. Teachers can review the worksheets to evaluate students' understanding of report content, market trends, and analysis.

This activity enhances reading comprehension and critical thinking skills by providing real-world examples of financial analyses. By analyzing stock market reports, students gain insight into market dynamics, investment strategies, and risk management techniques. This activity also promotes an understanding of the role of financial literacy in making informed investment decisions and managing personal finances.

Formal Letters

Objective: Enhance reading comprehension and writing skills by analyzing formal letters.

Level: Intermediate to Advanced

Duration: 60-75 minutes

Materials Needed

- Selection of formal letters from online sources
- Worksheet with questions related to letter content, structure, and language use

Teaching Outline

Introduction (5 minutes)

Begin by explaining the objective of the activity: to develop reading comprehension and writing skills by analyzing formal letters. Emphasize the importance of understanding the conventions of formal communication, including letter formatting, tone, and language use.

Instructions (5 minutes)

Distribute formal letters to each student or group. Provide a worksheet with questions related to letter content, structure, and language use.

Explain the task: students will read through the formal letters, answer questions, and discuss their findings with their peers.

Letter Analysis (40-50 minutes)

Allow students time to review the formal letters provided. Encourage them to analyze the purpose, audience, and tone of the letters, as well as the clarity and effectiveness of the communication. Prompt students to answer the questions on their worksheets and discuss their responses with their peers. Encourage students to consider the use of formal language, professional etiquette, and persuasive strategies in the letters.

Group Discussion (15-20 minutes)

Reconvene as a class and facilitate a group discussion. Allow students to share their interpretations and discuss the main features, strengths, and weaknesses highlighted in the formal letters. Encourage students to explore different approaches to formal communication and to consider the importance of clear and concise expression in professional contexts. Discuss the role of formal letters in business, government, and organizational settings.

Wrap-Up (5 minutes)

Summarize the key points discussed during the activity. Emphasize the value of analyzing formal letters for developing reading comprehension and writing skills. Encourage students to continue practicing formal communication techniques and to apply effective writing strategies in their own correspondence.

Assessment

Assessment for this activity can be based on students' completion of the worksheet and their participation in group discussions. Teachers can review the worksheets to evaluate students' understanding of letter content, structure, and language use in formal communication.

This activity enhances reading comprehension and writing skills by providing real-world examples of formal communication. By analyzing formal letters, students gain insight into professional writing conventions, etiquette, and persuasive techniques. This activity also promotes an understanding of the importance of effective communication in professional and organizational contexts.

Horoscopes

Objective: Develop reading comprehension and critical thinking skills by analyzing horoscopes.

Level: Beginner to Intermediate

Duration: 45-60 minutes

Materials Needed

- Collection of horoscopes (printed or digital)
- Worksheet with questions related to predictions, characteristics, and astrological signs

Teaching Outline

Introduction (5 minutes)

Begin by explaining the objective of the activity: to improve reading comprehension and critical thinking skills by analyzing horoscopes. Emphasize the cultural significance of horoscopes and their influence on people's beliefs and behaviors.

Instructions (5 minutes)

Distribute horoscopes to each student or group. Provide a worksheet with questions related to predictions, characteristics, and astrological signs. Explain the task: students will read the horoscopes, answer questions, and discuss their interpretations with their peers.

Horoscope Analysis (30-40 minutes)

Allow students time to read the horoscopes provided. Encourage them to analyze the predictions, characteristics, and astrological signs carefully. Prompt students to answer the questions on their worksheets and discuss their interpretations with their peers. Encourage students to consider factors such as relevance, accuracy, and personal beliefs in their analysis.

Group Discussion (10-15 minutes)

Reconvene as a class and facilitate a group discussion. Allow students to share their interpretations of the horoscopes and discuss their insights. Encourage students to explore different perspectives and interpretations, fostering critical thinking and analytical skills.

Wrap-Up (5 minutes)

Summarize the key points discussed during the activity. Emphasize the importance of critical reading skills in evaluating horoscopes and other forms of media. Encourage students to approach horoscopes with a skeptical mindset while also acknowledging their cultural significance.

Assessment

Assessment for this activity can be based on students' completion of the worksheet and their participation in group discussions. Teachers can

review the worksheets to evaluate students' understanding of predictions, characteristics, and astrological signs in the horoscopes.

This activity enhances reading comprehension and critical thinking skills by providing students with opportunities to analyze horoscopes. By examining predictions, characteristics, and astrological signs, students develop a deeper understanding of the cultural significance and influence of horoscopes on society. This activity also encourages collaboration and discussion, fostering a supportive learning environment where students can share their insights and perspectives on astrology.

Book Review

What did you think of *ESL Reading Activities for Kids and Adults*?

Please leave a review of the book on Amazon!

New ESL Books

Order new books via the *ESL Expat* website – or directly from Amazon.

Visit *ESL Expat* online for updated materials, new games, activity books and more resources for teaching English language learners.

ESLexpat.com

Made in United States
North Haven, CT
03 March 2025

66461316R00129